# The Eye In Team

## Morgan Eye

# The Eye In Team

©2019 by Hilltop30 Publishing Group, LLC

ISBN: 978-1-949616-04-0

Library of Congress Control Number: Pending

This is a work of nonfiction.

**To contact author Morgan Eye:**
Website: https://morganeye3.wixsite.com/mysite


**To contact Hilltop30 Publishers, LLC:**
Website: www.hilltop30.com
Email: tombrew@hilltop30.com
Phone: (727) 412-4008

For multiple copies of this book or to arrange book signings and/or speaking engagements, please feel free to email or call Hilltop30 Publishing Group, LLC.

Printed in the United States of America.

# DEDICATION

*I would like to dedicate this book to
my hometown of Montrose. Thank
you for making me who I am today.*

*Thank you for always being something
I could count on. This place and
the amazing people who make it
so great will always be home.*

*— Morgan*

Chapter

*"Contrary to popular belief, there most certainly
is an 'I' in 'TEAM.' It is the same 'I' that
appears three times in 'RESPONSIBILITY.' "*
— Amber Harding

**For many people,** there often can be one singular
moment that sums up what they're all about and how
they're wired. I have one of those, and I can't ever deny it
because my mother has it all caught on tape.

It goes way back, too. I was about three years old, and
when my aunt and uncle were about to get married, they
picked me to be a flower girl. On the day of the wedding,
I was supposed to get all dressed up and look pretty to do
my big job.

What you have to understand is that I was very much
a tomboy growing up in a tiny little town in Missouri. I
didn't want anything to do with looking pretty. I simply
wanted my hair pulled back in a ponytail, and I just wanted to wear my "yeans" — translation "jeans" in my little
three-year-old voice. A meltdown was coming, of course,
and as any great mom would do, she  captured my oh-so-
sad story on camera so I have full memories and visuals
to recall how the moment transpired.

My mom, my sister and I were at my Aunt Patty's
house in her beauty parlor, and everyone was getting
ready to get our hair done for the wedding later that
afternoon. My sister sat in the beauty chair getting her
hair curled while I waited sitting in the salon dryer chair.

My mom, with video camera in hand, asked me if I was going to get my hair done next. That's a bad question to ask a tomboy, especially with the camera rolling.

Mom and Aunt Patty teamed up on me and tried to coerce me into getting pretty for the wedding. My mom said, "You're going to be like Cinderella."

I was biting my bottom lip and shaking my head no. I still had a devilish smile on my face at this point, and it's plain as day on the video. I said the words softly while I was shaking my head, but you could hear them.

*"I ain't gonna be no Cinderella."*

*"I ain't gonna be no Cinderella."*

Of course you know what happens next. The video flashes forward to me sitting in the salon chair getting my hair curled, with my face as red as a fire hydrant, and tears streaming down my chubby cheeks. I was so upset, but a cookie did help calm me down.

And then I went out there and was the best flower girl I could be.

\*\*\*    \*\*\*    \*\*\*

**L**et's flash forward now. It's nearly fifteen years later and I am a senior in high school heading on my very first unofficial visit to the University of Missouri. My parents, my high school coach and I sat in on one of the basketball workouts that afternoon in the practice facility.

There was one other recruit on a visit with her parents as well. We sat along the wall in the practice gym watching the workouts. Missouri's head coach, Robin Pingeton,  sat between the other recruit and myself. Coach P went back and forth talking to me and the other recruit.

As she turned to talk to me, the first thing she did was give me a slight nudge and said, "Small town, huh? That would be a Cinderella story, wouldn't it?"

I looked at her with a shy smile and replied "Yeah…"
Turns out, I was a Cinderella after all.
So here is my Cinderella story.

# 2
## Chapter

**E**veryone has a story worth telling, but who will listen? Attention spans are fairly short these days. It is hard enough in today's society to have a two-minute engaged conversation with a person without someone quickly checking your phone for a text or social media alert.

Not everyone will want to get engrossed in me telling my story, but you're here now and that makes me happy. I'm only in my twenties, but I've already had a very interesting life. And I hope by telling my story of how a small-town girl — a *VERY* small-town girl — made it to the big time, that some other girl might get something out of it. If I impact just one person's life in even the smallest way, then this is a story worth telling. It's been fun living it — and it's even more fun telling you all about it.

My name is Morgan Eye, but in the college basketball world, almost everyone just calls me "Mo." I am still trying to figure out my passion and purpose in life. I don't know what God has lined up for me, but I do know it has to be something great because God doesn't know how to do anything short of that. I decided to write a book about my experiences in life, and most of that revolves around basketball and all the great things the game has brought me. Every time I think about my experience as a college basketball player, I think of it as a story of blessings. I am not the sports story of the kid who "made it" or went from "rags to riches." I am simply a small-town girl who had a really big dream, and I was given an amazing opportunity to live out that dream.

9

I have three purposes for writing about my experiences with basketball.

First, it's my hope that if just one person is positively affected by something that I write in this book, then I did my job.

Second, I hope that by being vulnerable and getting personal with the stories I share that others will relate to it and can benefit from what I've done when they go through similar experiences. I especially hope it helps other former athletes who are transitioning from being a student-athlete to something else, because it is a hard transition.

My third reason is mostly selfish. Writing down my experiences has been very therapeutic for me to finally reflect on all the blessings and struggles in my life.

This is me. All of it. I will bare my soul for you.

Are you ready? Let's go.

Chapter

**E**very sports buff loves numbers, stats and stories, so let me throw some figures at you to introduce myself. The first number is 384. That's the number of people in my hometown of Montrose, Missouri, which is located about an hour and a half south of Kansas City, and north of Springfield about an hour and a half.

As a small-town native, I get used to using other cities or towns to geographically explain to folks where exactly my hometown is, because it is that small. I honestly miss introducing myself as "Hi, my name is Morgan Eye, and I am from Montrose, Missouri. Oh don't worry, very few people know where it is. It's about 20 minutes from Clinton, Missouri." (I know. Most people don't know where Clinton is, either!)

I don't think I can put into words how much pride I have from where I come from. Montrose is more than just where I grew up. It is also a huge part of who I became as a person. Montrose is the type of town where people rally together to celebrate the good times, join together when loved ones are lost, and rally to follow a local girl in her quest to live out her dream of playing Division I basketball. I can't tell you how many times I would head to the bank in town or to our local Casey's General Store — our one and only gas station — when I was home from college, and someone would stop to ask me how school was going for me at the University of Missouri.

The next number is 12. That number represents my graduating class of 2011. I like to joke that the number is inflated because it includes our foreign exchange student, Sylvain Alberti. Another fun side note: Four people from my graduating class, including myself, attended the University of Missouri. For my sport-loving analytics people, that's approximately 33.33 percent of my entire class.

The final number is 1. That is the number of Division I basketball offers I received as a senior in high school. Luckily, it only takes that one offer, and it just so happened to be from the college I wanted to go to all along. When the University of Missouri offered me a scholarship, it gave me the chance to represent my home state, and not just my tiny little town. That meant the world to me, but I'm getting ahead of myself.

Let's go back to Montrose. That's where it all started, and that's where I got into position to eventually play for the Mizzou Lady Tigers. Let me lay out a little bit of my journey that got me to that position.

Here are the most important people who made that all happen for me:

*** *** ***

**MY DAD:** I guess anyone's journey would have to begin with two very important people — their parents. My dad's name is Kim Eye. Boy, was I so blessed with a unique last name like that, because newspaper headline writers have had a field day when writing articles about a gal who had an "eye" for the three-ball. My dad is a farmer, like his father before him, and has been all of his life. He farms row crops — soy beans, corn, and wheat. He has cattle and used to have hogs. His favorite farm story to tell is of the time one of his neighbors thought the Eye family had a tractor that could drive itself. My dad was about five years old at the time, well below the age to be driving or operating any sort of heavy machinery. (It should be noted that Dad may have embellished on his story through the years, but it's his story) But there he was, out there on the tractor, helping out on the family farm by plowing fields. He has been doing it all of his life, and I have loved every second of being able to call myself a farmer's daughter.

Growing up as a farm girl teaches you a lot of valuable lessons. I do want to set the record straight from the beginning that I would call myself a poor excuse for a farmer's daughter. For example, I never drove a tractor until I was in college. I always blame Dad for that, but really I think it was a great blessing that he gave both my sister and me the time to do what we loved instead of working on the farm all the time as kids. It allowed us to enjoy doing other things with friends, such as playing in countless summer leagues of basketball and softball. Those were my summers in Montrose, year after year.

At some point, I did have to embrace this whole "farmer's daughter" thing. One time I remember coming home from college and saying, "Dad, let's go drive the tractor because I'm tired of saying I grew up on a farm and have never driven a tractor." I had so much fun doing it that first time, mostly because I saw how my dad lit up when he was in his own element. He was telling me what all of the things on the tractor did, and when you should use it. Some of our equipment has been used gingerly over the years, and there are special ways to keep things running. My dad knows all those little tricks. I like to think it's just the character of the equipment.

My dad is a big history buff and oftentimes his stories can become a bit drawn out because he has to give you the history of every person in his story, whether you ask for it or not. As my basketball career blossomed, I was usually the subject of his stories. For a number of years, he reveled in sharing tales of his daughter playing basketball. I remember returning home during college and someone told me how my dad lights up when he shares a story about one of my college games and talks about how well I did.

I know my dad is very proud. When you walk into our two-car garage—or better known to our family as Dad's man cave—you can't get past the Morgan Eye memorabilia that covers the walls. I know my dad would be proud of me no matter what I decided to do in life, but I also know he absolutely loved watching me play basketball all these years.

I learned a lot of lessons from Dad, especially as it pertains to hard work. A farmer's work is never truly done. He has fields to tend to, livestock to check, and you just never know when those pieces of "character" farm equipment need some TLC. I remember as a kid how busy Dad got during planting and harvest season. You can always tell Dad means business when he zips through the driveway at unrecognizable speeds for him. He works crazy long hours, but he does what he has to do to get things done for our family.

I also learned another valuable lesson from my dad —teamwork. My dad does a lot of his farming with other local farmers, and they work together to yield the best harvest they can. I would say learning hard work and teamwork from my dad played a vital role with me growing up as I applied those skills to basketball—and to life.

**MY MOM:** My mom's name is Carla (Cook) Eye. Talk about one powerful woman. I learned a lot from my mom, too. She was always hard at work at West Central Missouri Community Action Agency, located in Appleton City, Missouri. She was employed there for fifteen years, twelve of those working with the Head Start Program. (Now she works at Osage Valley Electric Co-op in Butler as an administrative assistant.) We always enjoyed going to work with her as kids because we would bring movies and we got to do arts and crafts while we were there. We would make mom something and she would proudly display it in her office. My mom worked at countless fundraisers and did so many things for our school and church, all with the mindset of knowing she was doing it for her kids and the other kids in our tight-knit community.

I think another big thing I learned from my mom is to stand up for myself and not to always follow the crowd. My mom grew up in Montrose too, and she is strong-willed for sure. I love that about her. She also has the sweetest fun-loving side to her. A story her sisters — my aunts — always loved to tell was of the time when she was in her teens. At the grocery store, she randomly started bumping her cart into the aisles and singing loud to attract attention and embarrass her other sisters.

I remember a few things, too. I recall a time I had invited my cousins over for a play-date and my mom drove us all home from Grandma's house. As we approached the yard, she started making comments about how great the yard looked. She had just mowed it all, and just kept emphatically praising how good it looked. Next thing I knew, she started cutting donuts right in the yard. My cousins and I all slid against one another as she made each hard turn. We all got a real good laugh out of that.

I also learned discipline from my mom. I have this memory of my sister saying she finally realized why Mom always made us volunteer to be a server at mass at Immaculate Conception, our Catholic church. Every weekend, there are four servers on a list for that mass. But when someone doesn't show up, other kids are picked out of the congregation to serve. My sister and I always got picked, and we would serve five or six times consecutively. Mom always made us do it.

Years later, my sister was like, "Mom, now I know

why you always made us get up and go serve." I get it now, too. In life, sometimes we have to do things we may not feel like doing, but we do it because it is the right thing to do. Even more challenging is doing so with a gracious heart. We learned that from our mom.

**MY SISTER LAUREN:** I can't yet dive into my basketball experiences without talking about my role model, my older sister, Lauren. As a kid I wanted to do everything with her. It's funny, at her wedding—I was maid of honor—I joked how I was the annoying little tag-along sister, but here we are now, best friends. My sister always looked out for me, giving me little pieces of advice here and there. She was always the person who helped me keep my feet on the ground and helped me with keeping a level head.

Even if I had the game of a lifetime in high school, she would still point out something I needed to work on if something jumped out at her. She was my biggest fan, and always wanted to make sure I was as good a player as I could be. I respected her so much for always keeping me grounded. I needed someone like that in my corner to constantly push me and not to accept mediocrity.

I have always admired my sister's creativity and her drive. Lauren is now married and has two children. Her husband's name is Dan and their little boys are Renzy, whom we call Ren, and Roric. Everyone says Roric has a "sassy attitude" as a toddler like I used to have. I'll take that as a compliment! That's my buddy, right there.

Along with being a wife and mother, Lauren owns her own online boutique. This is my plug for her: Check out Rustic Honey, shoprustichoney.com and check out her blog at rustichoney.com. Seriously, this girl is a stay-at-home mom just down the road from Clinton, and she runs her own online business and manages a physical location of her store in her own shop at her house. When

I go to visit, I am always exhausted just playing with the boys, so I don't know how she does it. I certainly love my big sis—and to this day am always relying on her for advice.

**MY COUSIN TREVOR:** I can't recall the exact day I started playing basketball, but it's safe to say it has been as long as I can remember. My best friend growing up was my cousin, Trevor, and he was my running buddy at Grandma's house. I wanted to do anything and everything that he did—and that included taking off my shirt like the boys. I was quite the little tomboy back then.

If Trevor was playing football, then I was playing football. When Trevor started playing basketball, I started playing, and I found that I really liked it. My grandma babysat us growing up and it just so happened she lived right across the street from where we went to school at St. Mary's Catholic School.

It's the same school all of our parents went to, as well as my grandma. There was a playground and concrete basketball court right there at our fingertips. We would play there almost every day after school, and especially on Sunday after church when our families all went to Grandma's house for breakfast. I guess you could say it was the court I grew up on, at least until I would get one of my own at our house a few years later.

**MY UNCLE KENT AND MY COUSINS KENDALL AND KATELYN:** Montrose and basketball go together like peanut butter and jelly, and I only use that analogy because I love a classic PBJ. Because our town is so small, basketball is our main sport. We aren't big enough to have a football team. Baseball and softball were fun, but basketball was what people planned their schedules around.

I began playing organized basketball in third grade, and I was so lucky that my uncle, Kent Hart, coached our team. I got to play with two of my cousins (Kendall and

Katelyn) growing up, and all of my best friends. I remember going to practice and doing all the basic drills, and our
parents would come to our practices and sit in the bleachers catching up with one another. They would watch us
learn and get better literally right in front of their eyes. It
was a fun family thing.

The cool thing about being from a small town is that
you get to play on sports teams with your best friends.
Another really cool thing is that our parents all went to
school together, and they all loved getting to watch their
own kids grow up and play together. I think if you ask
me or any of my friends back home, some of our greatest
memories are of playing sports together—all of it, the
practices, games, summer leagues, and traveling. Ask our
parents the same thing, and they will tell you it was some
of the best times for them as well.

I have a lot of fond memories of growing up of playing basketball with my friends and cousins, and being
coached by my uncle. I learned a lot of valuable lessons
from him. I think a lot of what he taught stuck with me
more than he realized. He was a funny guy, and you
could tell he liked coaching us. He taught us a lot, but he
made us laugh, too. One time, he taught us to remember
the pick and roll. He literally acted like he was picking his
nose and would say, "pick" and then he would act like he
was rolling the booger, "roll." It was kind of gross, but it
worked to make a point for young kids. We remembered.

One of the best lessons I learned from him was that
he would tell us how we had to put in work on our own
time. My Uncle Kent, he had a full-time job and coached
us on his time and his dime. He had coached his older
kids, Brittany and Cameron, and was now coaching his
youngest, Kendall. The couple of times a week we could
get together to practice would not be enough if we wanted to really become good. I took this to heart. so I worked

18

on getting better all of the time at home and after school.

I remember one time we were talking about defense and he said, point blank, that defense is about heart. I remember him patting his chest and saying, "You've just got to want it." Those who have followed my career will say that I was never known for my lock-down defense, but I also hope that they will testify that I played with heart on defense. It was something that I really had to work on in order to get playing time at the college level.

I also remember a time Uncle Kent using Kendall and I as an example and asking why we are able to be successful. It was not because we were extremely quick or athletic. However, we were able to shoot the ball really well. So maybe that is part of the reason I have always taken pride in shooting the ball well. It was something that was within my control as long as I was willing to put the time in. My uncle instilled that work ethic in me, and I never minded practicing hard on my own to get better.

**COACH GIL HANLIN:** Gil Hanlin was an old-school kind of guy and he used to coach a lot of really good boys' teams at Montrose. He would come and coach us for a few weeks in the summers and would catch up with us on the road now and then.

I respected Coach Hanlin and his knowledge of the game so much. I absorbed everything he taught us like a sponge. I remember one day he was talking to us and explaining how once a player thinks they are the best they can be and know everything, that is when they start to decline. I really took that advice to heart, and it made me realize you had to always keep raising your ceiling.

He could be a crusty old guy sometimes when he was coaching us. If we didn't listen, we had to get in listening position, which meant to hold a push-up position while he talked. I have to call the boys out on that one, because they were in the listening position much more than we were. I could tell Coach Hanlin stories all day.

**COACH SCOTT IRELAND:** He was my high school coach and he pushed us hard to chase our dreams. Coach Ireland always has been very supportive of me, and he's done a lot of good things in Montrose. He had a great basketball mind, and we all trusted him. He coached both the boys' and girls' basketball teams, was athletic director, principal and superintendent.

No spoilers here, so read on.

# 4
Chapter

**T**here's a funny story about how my basket-ball career started. In our first organized game as little third-graders, we hosted a game in our gym against Warsaw. It was close the whole game, and going back and watching the old VHS tape always cracks up my friends and me to see how little we were and how much we still needed to learn.

The game came down to the final seconds. Warsaw took the lead late with a bucket and their team cheered and high-fived each other. (They celebrated like they had won the lottery every time they scored; we had a much smoother approach.)

After they scored, I looked up at the clock and there was about ten seconds remaining. My cousin Kendall in-bounded the ball to me, and I dribbled down the court as fast as I could. I got to about the fourth hash on the right side of the lane and took the jump shot.

Nothing but net.

I hit the game-winning shot in my very first game ever. I think I may have given a calm little fist pump. It was the first fist pump that would be seen many of times throughout my career.

*** *** ***

**W**e had a really good group of girls who could play. I recall a time sitting on the bleachers in the Mon-trose gymnasium as a young middle-schooler. Uncle Kent talked to us about setting a goal of becoming the first

Montrose team to ever go to state. We were just young kids, but I grabbed on to that dream.

If the people of Montrose had a dream, it was to take a basketball team to the state final four games. It was something that had never been done in the history of our little school. Many good boys and girls teams had come very close, but none had broken through the wall. The curse was the quarterfinal game to advance to state, where several Montrose teams had tried and failed to advance.

If a team before us was able to do it, that would be great, but I wanted to do it ourselves, whether we be the first to do it or not. I fell in love with the game of basketball and I wanted to squeeze everything out of it that I could. The seed was planted in our minds early that we wanted to achieve the goal of winning state.

We all had a lot of fun together, which is what is so great about playing with your best friends in a small town. We did it up in style, too, even as little grade-schoolers.

Uncle Kent worked full-time and coached us, and he also was very handy at fixing up cars and then re-selling

As kids, we loved traveling to basketball tournaments in our team limo, mostly because we could all be together on every ride.

them. All the girls loved traveling to the games together, and sometimes it was a problem getting us there if not enough parents could drive to road games. Uncle Kent set off in search for a van that he could fix up and we could travel in.

He did one better, though. He found a limousine for us to ride in. Talk about riding in style as grade-school girls. We thought we were pretty cool.

He fixed that limo up nice, too. He painted it all white, and it had black-tinted windows with a blue interior (our school colors), and blue lights on the inside. He hung trophies and plaques inside the limo, and the most personal touches were the words on the windows that read:

> Limo: $1200
> Repairs: endless
> Memories: priceless

We would ride off to our games, blaring the music and singing our hearts out. Whenever we played too much rap music, Kent would always holler to play some more of the Gretchen Wilson we had on hand. We became well known in our part of the state for the team that traveled in a white limousine to basketball games. It was always funny to see the expressions of people we drove past as they read the words on the limo.

When we were in fourth and fifth grade, our team rode on the limo in our Memorial Day Weekend parade, which is a big deal and a huge holiday celebration in Montrose. We rode in and on the limo through the parade with signs that hung from the sides of the limo that said "Future State Champs 2010."

I am sure we looked really cute as little youngsters, with our signs of becoming hopeful state champs. We were dreamers, and we were all about making dreams come true, too.

***   ***   ***

**I**t **was always fun** having Coach Hanlin around because he was such a legend and so well respected. He coached a lot of my friends' dads in high school. He would come to visit every few weekends to coach our team and the boys' team in grade school. For us girls, it helped a lot because when he was there we got to practice against the boys' team—and that meant I got to go toe-to-toe with my buddy, my cousin Trevor. It was always a good experience for us.

One weekend we traveled to a basketball tournament when we were in seventh or eighth grade. The tournament was near where Coach Hanlin lived, so he came to the games. Right in the middle of our game, all of a sudden we could see that Coach Hanlin was being tended to by a sea of people. It must have been an exciting game because it turned out he was having a heart attack over on the baseline.

We couldn't believe that happened during our game. The crazier thing was that he could have easily stayed home and no one would have been around to help him. We can easily joke now that because he came to watch us play, we probably saved his life. We went and visited him in the hospital the next day. Uncle Kent said Coach Hanlin was so impressed how every time he would speak, he could tell that all of us girls were listening intensely.

We respected Coach Hanlin and all of his wisdom. We were happy that he was alright. He taught me a lot of invaluable lessons and helped us grow when we were young. (Since then, Coach Hanlin actually made a return to Montrose and coached the 2016-2017 boys' basketball team. There is something about Montrose that tugs at the heart strings.)

*** *** ***

**M**y childhood is literally jam-packed full of memories that revolve around basketball. I really locked on to the game and fell in love with everything about it at a very early age. I would be in my basement watching basketball games, and during commercials I would dribble my ball all over. I would imagine dribbling through defenders as I worked my way around the pool table. I would take two dribbles toward the wall and just as I would come to the edge of the pool table, I would wrap the ball around my back as the announcers in my head explained each of my swift moves.

I learned a lot from watching basketball on television, too. I absorbed a lot of what the announcers talked about, which enhanced the personal commentating in my head when I would play around. That is one reason why I like to consider myself knowledgeable about a lot of sports. I am the girl who can legit talk sports and not just pretend that I know what I am talking about. I can talk football, baseball, and basketball all day. Listening to the announcers, you can learn a lot about the rules of the game. You can also hear them talk strategy and what they might do in certain situations. It allows you to immerse yourself into the game and think about what you might do in that particular instance. I would like to think a lot of what I learned from just watching the game helped prepare me for situations that I would also face later in my career.

As much as I don't condone playing video games for hours like my cousins and I would do, you can actually learn a lot from those as well. I would play Trevor all the time at Grandma's house. He was really good, so I can't recall winning a ton, especially in Madden, the football game. I would try to get fancy and utilize the hit stick, but he ended up juking me, leaving my avatar player looking all kinds of silly. He dominated me in Madden, and usually won a lot in baseball, but in basketball, I could give him a run for his money.

When we weren't playing sports on video games, we were physically playing sports. I got a small basketball hoop for one of my early birthdays, coincidentally from Uncle Kent. As I got older, I was always playing on it in our basement. It's one of those basketball hoops that you play with a small basketball. Keep in mind, my basement has the standard ceiling, which was only eight feet or so, maybe a little higher.

That may be why my shot was relatively flat when I got older. I played with my cousins all of the time. It was always me and Trevor versus Kendall and Katelyn, and we dominated every time we played anything against them. I'll go on the record defending that statement. We were the elder cousins, so we had to teach them a thing or two.

# 5
Chapter

**I**n my summer leading into high school, I took on the challenge of a jumping program. I am sure this sounds very humorous to people who have witnessed my vertical leap—or lack thereof—in action. One of my former coaches at Missouri, Michael Porter, used to give me a hard time at practice. We would be doing layups and he would joke that you could slide a piece of paper underneath my vertical.

But there was a time in high school that I could actually jump pretty well. There was a kid in my school who had an insane vertical, and he told me his vertical actually used to be even better after he did a specific jumping program. I decided to ask him if I could get a copy of the program. He gladly made copies and I began my sixteen-week jump program in the summer going into my freshman year in high school.

To begin, I had to mark where my vertical leap started. I marked my progress on the wall that led down the hallway to the bedrooms in our house. I remember the first time I was actually able to even touch that part of the wall, and I thought I was hot stuff. That would serve as a measuring stick to track my progress and final results.

The jumping program itself consisted of a series of exercises that targeted your legs and was to be performed three times a week. I was committed to the workouts in addition to my games and practices, so it made for a busy summer for me. Some weeks it took extra planning in advance if I had a game or would be traveling. Sometimes that meant going two or three days in a row, but I had to make sure I got all my workouts in.

My mom tells the story the best about the time she and my family were inside, and they watched me as I decided to get my jump workout done outside in the summer heat. I was dripping with sweat while I performed the series of jumping moves. She said my sister then came to the door and watched as I did my series of jumping moves off a wooden chair that I had dragged outside. I stepped one foot on the chair, elevated and switched feet in the air and landed on the other. I performed the move continuously, jumping and switching feet as fast as I could. As Lauren peered out, she said, "Mom, I love basketball, but not that much."

As I finally neared the end of my jump program, I remember telling Mom I really did not realize how long sixteen weeks was! I could have easily called it quits after two weeks, or eight or ten. No one was holding me accountable. No one dared me or challenged me to do it. I was just driven and focused to finish. I was hungry to see results. If this jump program promises you will add inches to your vertical, I wanted to prove I could do it.

The final day came, and I finished the program. The program recommends waiting a week to record your final vertical. As I approached the wall at the front of our hallway, I stared at the original piece of tape, I took my allotted one step into my jump and easily reached several inches above my initial mark. I don't have my actual recorded numbers, but this was a big achievement for me. I committed to doing something and I followed all the way through, and I saw results.

The same mindset would help me later on as I began my collegiate career.

# 6
Chapter

**A**s **high school finally** approached, I dove head first into all three of the sports that Montrose offered for girls. I played basketball and fall and spring softball. I ran cross country only because it was mandatory to get in shape for the basketball season. As much as I dreaded cross country, I learned a lot of mental toughness from it. It also was surprising that a lot of us were pretty good at it for not really investing a whole lot into it. I was a state qualifier all four years of my high school career. I can still recall the feeling I would get in my stomach as I would step to the starting line knowing I was about to run 3.1 miles — a feeling I don't really miss.

Every time I am up early on a cool, crisp morning, I am taken back to the high school days of a race early in the morning. When I first started running cross country, the idea of running 3.1 miles seemed impossible. I had never run that many miles at one time. What seemed impossible was merely only in my head. I wasn't passionate about cross country, but I was passionate about basketball and if I was told cross-country would help get me in shape, then I'd do it. Ironically, as a mid-20s former collegiate athlete, I LOVE to run now. I run almost every day. Working out is my "me time," and it just makes me feel good. I have run one half-marathon and am looking forward to running many more. My mom laughs every time when we reminisce about my high school days of me dreading running cross-country, because now I can't stop running.

I really enjoyed softball and miss it to this day. I grew

up playing T-ball in a co-ed league, which again meant I got to play with Trevor. He and I always played base-ball at Grandma's house. We would take turns being the pitcher and catcher. Four thrown balls earned a run for the other team and a strikeout meant an out for our invis-ible opponent. I wore my Kansas City Royals hat nearly every day, so much so that I can still hear my Grandma scolding me, "You're gonna lose all your hair if you keep wearing that hat!"

Our games in Grandma's front yard quickly got moved to the backyard after Trevor and I broke one of the front windows. No wild pitches were thrown, but on this particular day, we thought we would try to hit the ball, and it went right through a window.

In T-ball, I played pitcher, which meant I faked a pitch, the kid swung at the ball on the tee and it rolled to me and I made the routine throw over to Trevor at first base—just like how we did it at Grandma's house.

After T-ball, I moved up to Coach-pitch, and finally softball. Guess who coached my team? Yep, Uncle Kent. We always had a blast playing softball and our team was really good. We won multiple tournaments and district titles during our middle school and high school days. I always loved getting my jersey dirty. If I had the chance to slide, I was going to make sure I did it. Over the years I played catcher, pitcher, and shortstop. My main position was shortstop and I loved it because I felt like I was in on every play. I loved my softball days. I loved the weekends spent with my friends at tournaments and the school bus rides to games. My friends really are what made the expe-rience that much sweeter.

The rest of it was fun, but basketball was my passion. I always wanted to play basketball. It was what I was best at, too. I was a decent cross-country runner for not having passion for it. I was a pretty darn good softball player.

Basketball was what I was most confident at, and it's what I looked forward to doing the most.

My freshman year, we actually only had six girls — five freshmen and one sophomore who ended up getting hurt. It was a good learning experience and we had a great year, winning both our conference and district titles. I think we surprised a lot of other teams because Montrose had graduated their entire team the year prior (which included my sister, Lauren) and so there was not much expectation from outsiders. There was a preseason article that highlighted what to expect from our districts that upcoming season, and there was no mention of Montrose at all. Little did they know me and my squad had other plans. Only our team and parents who had been watching us our whole lives knew what we were capable of doing.

In high school, I played all five positions at various times. I was the tallest girl on the team at 5-foot-9, so I could play inside and out. We had a great bunch of girls. Kristin Bellinghausen and I went to school together all the way from kindergarten through graduating from Mizzou. She will be a bridesmaid in my wedding. I will be matron of honor at her upcoming wedding in the fall of 2019. Kristin played the post position. I'll always remember her being a right hander who was taught to shoot it left handed — but hey, it went in. Felicia Foster — we called her Flip — is a great friend and she's also a bridesmaid in my wedding. Flip was that teammate I pushed a lot, and sometimes I think she may have needed it. She was a good player and I knew we needed her to work hard. By our senior year, she was a very consistent three-point shooter for us. Kendall Hart, my cousin and another future bridesmaid, also could play all five spots. She matched me in height and she was very versatile. Growing up, Kendall was a point guard, but in high school she definitely used her size and strength to her advantage and had a textbook hook shot she used. She played the point when we needed her, because she could handle the pressure. She was a fantastic three-point shooter — and a half-court shooter, for that matter. Kendall went on to play at Rockhurst University. I was able to make it to one of her games before her career was over. I sported a sign that read, "#24 has my HART."

Katelyn Bracher (another cousin, another bridesmaid) was like a little gnat on defense. She was dubbed "The Glove" by our assistant coach, Tim Hankins. She always took on the toughest defensive assignments every game. She was a consistent three-point shooter and had the most unique style of shooting layups where it appeared as though she were flying. She took our jokes in stride. Victoria Engeman was a long, lanky player. She knew her role and did it to the fullest, often coming through in clutch situations. Elizabeth Collins became a strong defensive stopper for us by my senior year and could knock down the open three-pointer. Whitney Klass, the lone sophomore my freshman year, was like the mother hen of the team. Constant injuries kept Whitney on the sidelines a lot, but it never took away the value she brought to the team. Winning the conference and district titles were nice, but we fell short in the game that would advance us to the quarterfinals, which is one game from going to the final four.

I remember after losing the game that people kept giving us support and saying that we are so young, and we had three more years. I absolutely hated the excuse that we were young. Even at the age of fifteen, I felt like I should have been able to conquer the world on the hardwood. That freshman year, our team learned a lot and now we would finally gain the rest of our squad that had been playing with us all those summers, that class behind mine that included my cousins Kendall and Katelyn. Our team that had been together since second and third grade could finally pursue our dream of making a title run like we had always dreamed of.

We had surprised many opponents during our freshman season and now that we would have the rest of our team together, we were only gaining more firepower.

We were young, but we were pretty darn good already.

# 7
Chapter

**I have been asked** many times before who my basketball idols were growing up. It was kind of hard to answer that question because I think there are so many talented players that emerge every year, and you just want to take a little from everyone's game.

As a young kid, I loved Michael Jordan. Unfortunately, I was born in 1992, so I would be far too young to remember his glory days. I do recall watching him play for the Washington Wizards at the end of his NBA career. MJ is a legend, so it doesn't take long for a basketball junkie to understand his relevance to the game. I loved his passion for the game and I think that was something I always thought was amazing.

There was also a Montrose girls basketball legend who I idolized growing up, Tina McClain. She played in the early 1990s at Montrose, again around the time I was born. I think she deserves a lot of credit for making girls basketball in Montrose relevant. I remember Mom telling me how she had the smoothest shot and how she could play with the boys — I believe Mom's words were "poetry in motion." She was the first player from Montrose to go on to play Division I basketball. She played for the Nebraska Cornhuskers. She left her mark at Montrose, leading them to multiple tournament titles and holding the scoring record for girls with over 2,300 points.

Even though I had never met the woman, I knew who she was and everyone from Montrose certainly knew, too. People would talk all the time about how good she was and they recalled how people from home would take bus loads to go cheer her on at Nebraska. To this day, I have never seen any film on Tina McClain, nor have I even met her, but I thank her for being a big part of my motivation to get better and better.

One Christmas, when I was probably a freshman in high school, we were in our basement at home going through our stockings. Santa always put lots of great stuff in there—sweets, mints, gum, makeup, movies, little gadgets, etc. This Christmas, I had a little tin box in my stocking. I took the lid off of the tin box to find a small card. It was a Nebraska Cornhuskers women's basketball schedule from 1996 featuring Tina McClain on one side and their schedule on the other.

It was like having my own playing card of Tina McClain—a rookie card, if you will. I was so pumped! Dad was the one who had kept the card for years and he thought I would really enjoy having it, and he was right. As much as Mom gives Dad a hard time about never throwing anything away, sometimes hidden gems do come in handy.

The third person who motivated me as a kid was another small-town girl, Jordan Garrison from Osceola, Missouri. I never really knew Jordan all that well, but we would eventually play against each other numerous times in high school and once even at the collegiate level. Basketball is really big around Montrose and the surrounding areas, so you obviously hear about this girl from a small-town getting looks from Division I schools. That's how it was with Jordan.

I remember always hearing so many people talking up Jordan Garrison, and I remember thinking that I really needed to work hard to keep up so I could eventually have my shot at playing Division I basketball, too. People were always talking about how many hours she would put in, and it made me want to do more.

I never liked the idea of someone working harder than me or putting in more work than me. That never meant that I would always win, but it meant that I would always give my best.

# 8
Chapter

**M**y **sophomore season** was a very good learning experience. We dominated a lot of the competition we faced. However, for me, it was never about just winning the game. We could handle a team by twenty or even thiry points, but if our team didn't play to what I felt was up to our standards, I would get upset.

I knew we could blow out a lot of the 1A schools that we faced, but this was about us being the best that we could be. It was about preparing us to win a state title for our school and our town.

The most competitive regular season games for us came against a 2A school, Osceola, where Jordan Garrison went. Osceola had a really good squad all four years we played them. We were each other's best competition in the regular season, so we always enjoyed the opportunity to play each other.

Montrose's gymnasium is very small, as you would expect. On games when it was our turn to host, we actually had bleachers from our city ballpark moved into the gym on the stage and north entry doors for more seating. I loved the competition, I loved the pressure, I loved that we had to bring our best game in order to come out on top. We didn't always win, but we became a better team with those types of games.

We actually advanced to the quarterfinal game my sophomore season, where we lost to Exeter, the eventual state champs. They were very good and had a girl with last name of Eddy who went on to play at Missouri State. I scored 1,000 points that season, and I was now hungrier than ever to get better.

But it was also stressful for me too, because I came home crying a lot thinking I had to do as much coaching as I was playing, and that I couldn't focus enough on improving my own game because I was having to help the others so much. So when it was decided that Coach Scott Ireland would coach our team fulltime, I was very, very happy. I knew we could get over this hurdle with him coaching us. I always liked and respected Coach Ireland and loved his family. He and his wife and their twin boys actually rented my grandpa's house. My first two years had been pretty good, but now I was ready to do more.

So much more.

# 9
Chapter

**M**y junior year, we really felt like it would be our year to win state. We had age and experience on our side now and had already played in big games with pressure. We had fallen short in the sectional game my freshman year and then made it a step further my sophomore year—losing in the cursed quarterfinal game. Now it was time for us to go farther.

It was a dominant season for us, and we once again owned our conference and district, both during the regular season and in the tournaments and were undefeated. Then we easily handled the sectional game to advance us to the state quarterfinal game for the second-time in my career.

Verona was our quarterfinal opponent. That round of the tournament had cursed Montrose for years. No team had been able to break down the brick wall that would allow for a final four berth. The game against Verona was probably my most memorable high school game. I remember preparing for the game in the days leading up to it. Coach Ireland had us watch film on them. They had three girls who did the majority of their scoring. We would need to key in on them, specifically defensively. I remember being at home in my basement, again dribbling my ball around the basement—I did this even in high school—and I really worked on my crossover dribble between the legs to make sure that when I went from one hand to the other between my legs that I didn't expose the ball so it could get stolen.

I kept working on it until I felt more comfortable. I even went into our guest bedroom and grabbed a full-length mirror so I could see that I was protecting the ball as I crossed over. Using a mirror really helped me so that I could see what I looked like to a defender, and that I wasn't vulnerable to getting the ball stolen from me.

Game day finally arrived, and we played the game at State Fair Community College in Sedalia, Missouri. Before our bus left for games, we always tried to get to the gym a little early so we could shoot around and get comfortable. This was something we did before most road games. Any time I could get some extra shooting in, I was going to do it. For me, it was never necessarily getting up a ton of shots, but being intentional about my shooting. It was more about whether my shot felt good.

Did it feel smooth coming off my fingertips? Was I swishing my shots or were they clanking in? I also practiced shots that I knew I would be getting in games. I worked on layups, jump shots, free throws, three-pointers, everything. After shooting in our gym for a bit, it was time to load onto the bus and head to the game.

I'll be honest; I can't remember a ton from the game itself. I will say the same thing about my more recent college games. I remember bits and pieces, but when your adrenaline is running and you get in a zone, it is hard to explain how you did certain things or what you were even thinking during that time. I do remember going into halftime, though. We had a slight advantage on Verona, up only a few points. I had been held to just a couple points in the first half and I just remember coming out of the locker room for the second half and thinking "Not this year, no way, I'm not letting us lose."

We came out firing in the second half. I scored 29 points myself in the second half, and I remember a key possession. I scored a quick basket, and then acted like I was heading back on defense, only to quickly turn back and snag the inbounds pass for a quick layup. That was four quick points.

The buzzer finally sounded, and my teammates and I all ran to each other and hugged. We had broken the curse. We lined up for pictures underneath the basket for our parents. That's when the emotions got real. As I looked out to our parents and the other fans remaining in the stands watching us, I couldn't help but get emotional. All of our parents were in front of us, cameras in hand, and flashes were coming from everywhere.

We had huge smiles on our faces. Through our smiles, we were talking to one another, "Who do we look at?" Seeing our parents fighting back tears and hugging one another brought a whole new level of emotion into play. Our school, our town, wanted this so bad and we were able to help give them that. We were going to state!

We headed back to the locker room still on a high. I remember hugging everyone and the tears just started flowing. I remember saying, "I've never cried after winning a basketball game." I was so moved by this game. It was literally one of the best feelings after a win that I have ever felt. There is only one other game that I have been moved to tears by pure joy and happiness after winning, and that happened later in college.

We were heading to state for the first time in Montrose High School history, and it felt so good.

# 10
Chapter

The Class 1A state final four games were played in Columbia at Mizzou Arena on the campus of the University of Missouri. For now, I was a Montrose Bluejay about to play in the Tigers' arena and, at the time, I had no idea it would become my home for four years in college. The thought had never crossed my mind. Not then.

I have to be honest, the final four games just felt like icing on the cake to me after finally clearing that hurdle in the quarterfinal game. I was super confident headed into the games. Having won in the quarterfinals, I felt like we had already won the state title and this was just a gift to get to play some more basketball. Of course, when it came time to play, I recovered my killer mindset and was ready to take it to our opponent to get the title we had worked so hard for.

Playing in the final four didn't mean we would change anything from what we were doing. All of the work we had put in over the years was paying off and it was time to just let it shine. We did not have to do anything different but play our game.

As the day arrived to head to Columbia, our school had a pep rally assembly to send us off. Not only was there a pep rally, but you should have seen the school spirit everywhere in town. Like I've said, little Montrose lives for basketball. It was very common prior to our big games for signs and decorations to be everywhere, including signs along the road on our way to our destination. Our parents took the time to make signs and drive the day before to put them up so that we could see signs of encouragement all along our way to Columbia.

If you drove down the main street of our town, you would see storefronts with blue-and-white window paint and Bluejays decorations in the front. One of my favorite signs was the one in the front of Kendall's house that read, "Just two itty-bitty games left."

I think my Uncle Kent was the one who started that during our district games. After a victory, he would say just "six itty-bitty games left … just five itty-bitty games left." That kind of became our mantra moving on from districts because when you look at the games you have remaining to winning a title, it is only four — sectionals, quarterfinals, state semifinals, and the championship game.

We had cut the list from four itty-bitty games left to two itty-bitty games left. One of the coolest signs had been used for years when other Montrose teams headed out of town for big games. It said, "Last one out of town shut off the lights!" That was no joke because EVERYONE from our town was not going to miss the chance to see us make history.

A reporter from the Channel 9 television station in Kansas City also made its way to our school to do a story on our team. I was interviewed by Maria Antonio, someone who I often saw on the news when I was at home and Mom and Dad had the morning or evening news on TV.

I remember how nervous I was for the interview. My palms were sweaty, as always, and when it was all over, I remember feeling that I stumbled over my words a bit. Luckily, they edit most of that stuff, so the final story ended up being pretty good.

The day before our semifinal game, we got to practice in Mizzou's practice facility. Of course, we were all in awe of everything and we snapped a lot of pictures. Then as we began practice, I remember starting to feel a lot of fatigue and thinking, "Man, this court is huge!" It felt so much longer than a high school court, which in fact it was, but not by that much.

Our semifinal game would actually be played in the historic Hearnes Arena, which was where the Missouri basketball teams played for a long time before Mizzou Arena was built in 2004. That didn't bother us at all, because we had actually played in Hearnes in the Show-Me Games, so we were somewhat familiar with it.

Naylor was our semifinal opponent. They had some really big girls on that team, but it didn't matter when we started raining three-pointers on them and putting on full-court pressure. We controlled the game easily from start to finish and even tied a record for most three-pointers (12) made in a state game. It was a great team victory.

Now we were one itty-bitty game away from a state championship.

One itty-bitty game.

# 11

Chapter

**T**he state championship game would be played on the Mizzou Arena court. A huge snow and ice storm blew in that evening, but you would have never guessed it because our fans still made the trip in full force to support us. Most everyone from Montrose came, and so did lots of fans from neighboring towns to support us as well.

I remember the arena feeling so big as we started our warmups. Even the lights from the ceiling seemed blinding when going up for reverse layups. This was a big-time college arena and quite a bit bigger than our small gym back home. It may have been a worker at the state games or somebody else, but they asked us if we had seen the movie "Hoosiers."

I was embarrassed to say at the time that I had never watched the movie all the way through. This gentleman thought our team was just like the Hickory team in "Hoosiers." There is a great scene in the movie where the coach takes out a tape measure to show that the distance from the basket to the free throw line and to the rim was the same distance as their tiny gym at home as it was on the big arena floor the Hickory Hoosiers would be playing on. I have since seen the movie in its entirety and do see a striking similarity to our Montrose Bluejays team.

When it was finally time for the starting lineups to be announced, we got to watch a highlight video from our semifinal game. The video featured both teams in the final game up on the giant JumboTron video screen. That video really got us fired up and even cracking a smile or two.

The ball was tipped and we were off.

I have to be honest, I don't recall many of the possessions from that special game. I do remember that we struggled more than we should have because we definitely felt that we were the far better team. We had to make an adjustment from playing man-to-man defense to a zone. We were used to playing mostly man-to-man, but we needed to shake things up and it ended up paying off.

As I mentioned earlier, I always held myself and my team to high standards. It was never about just winning, but I wanted us to always play to the best of our ability. I recall a specific instance toward the end of the game. We had not played our best at all, but we had a comfortable lead with only seconds remaining. One of our girls was shooting a free throw and my cousin Katelyn and I were waiting behind the three-point line. I remember Katelyn had a look on her face like she was upset about the previous play or maybe I even jumped on her for something. It was not uncommon for me to call out my teammates for something, but that just came with demanding the best from myself, and from them. They all understood.

At the end of games, I always made sure to follow up with them to make sure we were good. They knew how competitive I get, so it was never an issue. Anyway, whatever made her seem down, I looked to her, knowing we were about to win the state title and not wanting that moment to be spoiled.

I smiled and said, "I'm going to Disney World," like they do after the Super Bowl. She may have tried to force a smile. As we heard the buzzer sound, we ran to one another jumping and hugging in celebration. Felicia actually tried to jump into Kristin's arms and fell to the floor, but it didn't matter — it made for a funny story later. We were so excited. The dream we had as little second- and third-graders had come true.

The medal ceremony was very special. The head of MSHSSA went down the line as each of our names was announced and we tipped our head as the medal was placed around our necks. As captains, Felicia and I accepted the Class 1A state championship trophy. We went to hoist it high above our heads for our fans to enjoy, but Felicia quickly yelped because I was quite a bit taller than her and she couldn't hoist it that high. We still made sure to show off that puppy, though.

We headed to the locker room, where we proceeded to take tons and tons of pictures. We were all on such a high that we were just snapping as many pics as we could. Then, as Coach Ireland and Coach Hankins came to the locker room, we presented Coach with a WWE wrestling belt that we had bought for him. He joked one time at Walmart about how if we won he would need to get one. We secretly had one of our parents pick one up on the off chance that we did indeed win. It was a good extra surprise.

As we changed out of our uniforms, we made our way to the main concourse, where a sea of blue awaited to give hugs and take even more pictures. I don't know if I ever verbalized it, but when I hugged my Uncle Kent, there was an extra special-ness to the hug, as if to say, "Thank you. Thank you for everything that you have done for us girls. Thank you for your time and dedication to us. We did it!"

We headed for home the next day after winning. I'm not sure anyone got much sleep with the high we were all on, our parents included.

When we finally won our state championship, it was the culmination of a dream we all had since we were second- and third-graders. It felt so good!

We have a tradition on bus rides home from every away game that we sing our school song. Win or lose, we always sing our song.

As the bus approached the city limit sign "Montrose population: 417" (now its 384), I whipped out my camera to record our singing:

> *Three Cheers for our dear ol' high*
> *May the spirit of her never die*
> *Boost our colors of blue and white*
> *Forward on with all our might*
> *Let us make her the best in the state, ALRIGHT*
> *Write her name on every slate*
> *Boost our teams, win our games, study too*
> *Dear Montrose High, dear Montrose High,*
> *now here's to you*
> *M-M-M-O-N-T-T-T-R-O-O-O-S-E*
> *M-O-N-T-R-O-S-E*
> *MONTROSE!!!*

The moment when I got to proudly sing the words "Let us make her the best in the state!" was an amazing moment for me. I remember singing that part especially loud. You remember singing that song on the bus so many times as a manager in junior high, and then as a freshman and sophomore, and you just wanted to make your team the best in the state.

We had finally done it!

As the bus pulled into our parking lot, we had another surprise. After the big snowstorm, several fans thought, "We've got to do something for these girls." As we got closer, we saw a big "#1" made out of snow and blue food coloring added for our school colors. This thing was huge.

It was so cool and we jumped right over to the "#1"

and got our picture with it. The pride that Montrose has for its basketball is real.

# 12
### Chapter

After we won state, we got to do so many cool things. We had our own reception at our gym. We had t-shirts made that proudly said STATE CHAMPS 31-0. We signed so many T-shirts that day, it was like we were celebrities. It really was a special thing for us to win state for our town that had longed to go to the final four all those years. We were able to do one better and bring home a championship. That trophy was proudly displayed in the middle of the trophy case at school right in the hall where you first walk in the doors. I still smile to this day every time I see it.

We got to visit the state capitol and be announced in front of the House and Senate. It was a fun day visiting our capitol and, I must say, for some basketball gals, we cleaned up very nicely.

We visited the rotary club in Clinton, where we were recognized for our achievement. They also announced that they wanted us to serve as the Grand Marshalls of their Fourth of July parade. Of course, we accepted.

Memorial Day weekend rolled around again. We had our own float for the parade that our parents worked so hard on. We all rode on a wagon, four girls on each side with our coaches. Behind us was a blown-up old photograph of our team riding on the limo years ago as fourth- and fifth-graders in the parade and the signs on the limo reading "Future State Champs 2010."

The words MISSION ACCOMPLISHED were added to the blown-up photo. There we were, 2010 and we were state champions! As the parade proceeded, we made it to the middle of our main street, where we were presented our state rings. Those rings were paid for by donations from members of our community, who donated money at our reception. That meant the world to us girls that the people of Montrose were willing to do that for us.

It was also revealed to us that a new banner would proudly be displayed every Memorial Day Weekend in Montrose. The banner read: Welcome to Montrose. Home of the State Champion Lady Blue Jays 2010. It's a humbling reminder every time I see that sign when I am home for the parade. I smile a good smile, and remember why I so much love where I grew up.

***   ***   ***

The overwhelming number of congratulatory messages from everyone after winning the state title was incredible. There was one text from Travis Munsterman that I still think about to this day. He was about five years older than me. He was a part of one of the best boys basketball teams that came out of Montrose. My opinion may be a bit biased because my cousin Cameron — who is Kendall's older brother — was on that team and they were coached by my uncle Kent when they were growing up as well.

They were the team that everyone thought was going to "break the curse." I thought they would, too. They came so close and I know how bad they wanted it. I can't tell you word for word what the text read, but I remember it being along the lines of him thanking me. He felt that it made up for them not being able to make it to state when they had their opportunity.

I think this memory stuck with me because it makes you realize how much passion the people of our town have for basketball — not just basketball, but for where you come from. You do your best to make the people who care for you proud of you.

I know for a fact, win or lose, our community will always be proud. It's just really hard to realize that as a player sometimes.

Chapter

**Y**our senior year in high school is always a tough thing to go through. It is your year of lasts, and it can become really emotional if you allow yourself to go down that road. My senior year was going to be exciting too, as our team looked to repeat as state champions and I would hopefully decide where I was going to college.

College recruiting was very different for me because I never played on an AAU basketball team during the summers. Instead, I played with the same group of girls from second and third grade and all through high school. The AAU circuit is probably the best way for players to get noticed by colleges—especially the big schools. We did play in a lot of competitive leagues against AAU teams, so I was definitely getting better against really good competition. But it definitely wasn't the AAU grind. I played with my friends, and I preferred that.

Summer basketball was always the best basketball because our team, even though we were all from a tiny town, was really good. My favorite games would be when we would be warming up and the other team would give us a once-over and the looks on their faces said it all, "That's who we are playing?" We didn't have any fancy name-brand gear. We wore your typical reversible blue and white jerseys with numbers on them. Kendall and I were the tallest at 5-foot-9, so I guess I could see why teams would have a tendency to look past us. These teams would all walk in with their fancy team name jerseys and matching gym bags. None of that mattered once the ball was tipped, and we would blow out some really good teams. We also got our rear kicked too every once in a while, but those games were where we learned a lot and that helped us get better. I remember Uncle Kent always telling us that we learned more from getting blown out than winning big. We needed the competition as a team, and I needed the competition myself if I wanted to play at the next level.

As I mentioned earlier, Uncle Kent also has a full-time job. He is a UPS truck driver. While on one of his routes, he made a stop at a gas station and a complete stranger recognized him from the previous weekend's junior high basketball tournament we had played in. The man asked Kent if he was the coach of the Montrose girls and proceeded to tell Kent that he had seen our championship game against the X-plosions. They were, what we called, a "cream of the crop" team made up of hand-picked talented girls around their area. I remember their beautifully colored green jerseys and how they all walked around so confidently. They had a girl who just towered over us, but we didn't care.

I lived for those types of games where I knew the other team thought they would destroy us. The man continued his story by telling Kent he was watching both teams warm up and he nudged his wife and sarcastically said, "This should be a good game." He did not think we had a chance. Then he gained more excitement in his voice as he told Kent, "Your girls can play!" Like I said, we may not have looked the part, but we could play. We had a chemistry that can be attributed to the true friendships we had with one another. We blew out the X-plosions that day for the tournament championship.

One tournament we entered, we could not use our school name, so Kent got creative and named us the Hicks from the Sticks. He thought it was funny how the further we advanced in the tournament, people would be reading the bracket and they'd say, "Those Hicks from the Sticks are still in it!" It really was the perfect name for us. We were just a group of small-town girls who could ball.

*** *** ***

The downside to not playing on an AAU team was the lack of exposure to college coaches to recruit me. I know for a time Uncle Kent felt bad and wondered if he should have had me play on an AAU team so I would get more offers to play. I was entering my senior season and had no offers from any Division I programs, and no other offers from smaller schools that were appealing to me.

I was recruited by a few smaller schools in the Missouri area such as Northwest Missouri in Maryville, Lake of the Ozarks University, and a few others. None really met what I was looking for and I still wanted to pursue Division I. So what do you do when you are not getting noticed? You create your own opportunity—and luck.

I worked with my business teacher, Robyn Eckhoff, and we put together a highlight reel of my high school games. We sent them to three Division I schools: The University of Kansas, Kansas State, and the University of Missouri. I had been to camps at Mizzou before, but those camps were under the direction of former coach Cindy Stein. I had actually begun building a relationship with the staff my freshman year after I was named to an all-star team at one of the Mizzou camps. I remember the day Kendall and I arrived to camp, one of the assistants immediately greeted me with a handshake and said, "Morgan Eye, right?" I felt so shocked that the woman knew my name. It definitely made an impression on me. However, any relationship being built all but fell through because Mizzou now had a completely new coaching staff in 2011.

I also went to camps at Missouri State going into

my senior year. I really enjoyed the staff and players. I thought I could really see myself playing at Missouri State because Springfield was only an hour and 20 minutes from my hometown. A ton of my friends were already there in Springfield for college, so I would have a ton of friends around too. But Missouri State never showed interest in me, which surprised me. Maybe I didn't do so well at camp, or their scholarship numbers were low. I never knew why.

There was another college in Springfield to be considered though—Drury University. Drury was a small Division II school, but they had success on the national stage. They also had an amazing fan base, including Brad Pitt's mother, who came to all the home games. They were ranked nationally, played tough defense, and it was close to home. It was D-II, but I needed to check out all of my options in case my dream of playing Division I ball would not be possible. Coach Ireland sent my tape to Drury as well.

*** *** ***

**M**y friends and I played in a softball league in El Dorado, Missouri, almost every summer in high school. We were a darn good softball team, too. One time after heading home from a softball game in El Dorado, I checked my phone on the ride home and saw an unfamiliar number and a voicemail. I listened to the message on my super cool Blackberry Pearl, and remember it like this: "Hi, Morgan, this is assistant coach Randy Norton with the University of Missouri women's basketball team. We watched your highlight tape that you sent and I would like to talk to you more."

As soon as the words 'University of Missouri' came out of his mouth, I said, "Wait, what did he say?" I could not believe that Mizzou was calling me and wanted to talk some more after watching film on me.

On the day I had to call Coach Norton back, I was beyond nervous. I had sweaty palms and my heart was racing as I waited for someone to answer. He answered and asked me what I felt like I could do on the court. I answered as honestly as possible. I felt like I could shoot the ball, handle the ball, get to the rim, and dish the ball. One conversation led to another, and then eventually I talked with Missouri head coach Robin Pingeton. We set up a time for me to come to Mizzou for an unofficial visit.

Willie Cox, an assistant at Missouri, was the coach who got the honor of coming to Montrose to watch me in open gym. At the time of my senior year in high school, I didn't know him, but would get to know him better in the coming years. He would always joke with me about that first trip to Montrose. "Hey, Mo, what was that gas station? Casey's?" he'd ask. I always replied with a, "Yep, the only gas station in town." He loved to remind me of the day he came to watch me and made a quick stop at Casey's. He told me a lovely lady at the cash register gave him a quick history lesson on Montrose basketball. I always tell him, "That was probably Ada!" Her son wrote a book on the history of Montrose basketball. Ada always kept up with my basketball career and any time I was home visiting and my cousins and friends made our stop at Casey's, she would always ask how we all were and give us a quick, "Stay out of trouble." We always listened.

I don't recall being nervous or anything scrimmaging in front of Coach Cox. My girls and I played against some of the boys, and our assistant coach, Tim Hankins, guarded me. I did well. Nothing spectacular, but I played solid and showed what I could do. Because of NCAA compliance rules, I wasn't able to speak with Coach Cox personally, but my coach was able to speak with him before he left. I didn't know what he thought about me at the time, but years later — I think after I graduated from college — my coaches told me he came back and said, "Sign her."

I like to imagine he said it as smooth as he always talks — I believe everyone refers to it as "Willie-Style."

*** *** ***

On a September day, I took my unofficial visit to the University of Missouri. Mom, Dad, Coach Ireland, and I all hopped into Mom's car and made the little two-hour trek to Columbia. I was excited and nervous.

As we approached Mizzou Arena, we parked in the lot that the coaches directed us to. We made our way to the arena doors and were greeted outside by some of the coaching staff. I put my hand out to shake hands, but quickly put it down as I was embraced with hugs and told, "We're huggers." Assistant coach Jenny Putnam showed me around Mizzou Arena, the athletics facilities, and campus.

I got to watch the individual workouts of some of the Mizzou players. Coach Putnam led my family and I down the hallway toward the practice gym doors. I met a few of the players on the way to the floor. Coach Putnam introduced us and tried to brag on me a little. She told one of the Mizzou players how my team won state just last year. The player was like, "Oh really, what class?" I responded with, "1A." She literally went, "Psssh," and rolled her eyes right in front of my face. It was an awkward moment, but I quickly shrugged it off. I was used to people not thinking small-town girls could play. I'm sure Coach Putnam found the moment just as awkward, because I know that kind of behavior was not a reflection of the culture they were just beginning to build as they began their first year at Mizzou.

I sat in the practice gym along the wall in some folding chairs. Mom, Dad, and Coach Ireland all sat to my right. There was one other girl also on an unofficial visit. She and her family sat to our left. There was a small group of players — about four — being put through drills by the assistant coaches. I watched very intently. There were five cones lined up from the wing to the basket. Each girl took their turn performing the specific dribble move requested by the coach. The assistant barked out, "Between the legs, cross, and finish with a Rondo." The girls were pretty athletic as they made the moves. I sat there watching and just thinking to myself, "I can do that." Nothing that they were doing seemed out of my league at all. In that moment, I knew I could hang with these girls. My confidence was not shaken at all by watching the individual workouts that day.

Moments later Missouri head coach Robin Pingeton walked into the practice facility. Coach P — that's what everyone called her — sat smack dab between me and the other recruit. There was just something about this woman that you could feel when she entered a room. There was a confidence about her that made it obvious, even to those who may not have recognized her, but you just knew she was the head coach.

I don't want that to be confused with arrogance because Coach P is as far from that as you can get. You just had a sense that there was something real and genuine about this lady. Coach P went back and forth talking to me and the other recruit. One of the first things she did as she turned to talk to me, she gave me a slight nudge and said, "Small town, huh? That would be a Cinderella story, wouldn't it?" I replied in my shy way with a smile and a, "Yeah …"

The last part of my visit involved my family and I having one-on-one time with Coach P. She laid out exactly who she is, what she is about, and how she was going to build her program. I remember her saying, "It's faith, family, school, and then basketball." My mom made comments afterward about how Coach P really emphasized faith as being important. I think that was an important piece since faith is very important to my family as well. Coach P said between her and her staff, there were a lot of young kids and so it was very common to walk up to the offices and see a ton of kids running around. I liked picturing that type of atmosphere. It made it feel less intimidating and more like home.

During the meeting, we mentioned to Coach P that I had a sister who attended Stephens College in Columbia. She was like, "Oh, call her. She should come by." I remember my sister finally calling Dad back in the middle of our talk and Dad's conversation kept going on and on with Lauren. I was thinking, "Okay Dad, hang up the phone." I think Mom or me finally said something and I kind of had a look with big eyes of embarrassment, but Coach P just looked at me and gave me a wink. I did not want her to think we were rude, but she totally understood and that little wink said it all.

School was obviously a top priority for Coach P as well. There were no excuses for ever missing a class or tutoring appointment. As for the basketball part, she explained how it would be a tough process. Her and her staff were essentially taking over a program and building it from the ground up. She talked so much about how special it could be to come in and put in the work, be a part of the program growing, and finally see the fruits of your labor. That got me really excited. Why would I not want to be a part of something so special? I also remember her saying how you would meet girls who would become your best friends and eventually even be in your wedding. That comment really surprised me, and I kind of shrugged it off as something impossible. I already had such great friends that I had known since before kindergarten. How in the world would I ever experience greater friendships than that?

We left for home after our meeting with Coach P feeling really good. I was excited about the visit and was hoping that I would continue to talk with Coach P and hopefully get a scholarship offer.

Looking back at my recruiting process with Mizzou, I really enjoyed how they did it. I don't know if it was strategically planned this way or not, or if other recruits required attention from certain coaches, but I loved the layout of how each coach made contact with me in some way. It began with Coach Norton reaching out on the phone. I continued to talk with both him and Coach P on the phone. Coach Cox came to an open gym, and then Coach Putnam showed me around campus. I enjoyed lunch with the entire staff on campus and then, of course, finished with a conversation with Coach P. It meant a lot that I got to spend time with each of the members on the staff. I think it showed my parents and I that they truly cared about making my visit a good one, whether or not at the time they were serious about asking me to attend Mizzou.

\*\*\* \*\*\* \*\*\*

The only other visit I took was to Drury University in Springfield. When I first spoke to head coach Steve Harold on the phone, he was very impressed with my highlight tape that I had sent in. He asked me what other schools were looking at me. Many other smaller colleges would ask me the same thing. I would give them the list and always end with, "And the University of Missouri." Most of the time that led the coach on the other line saying, "Who?" and I would reply, "Mizzou." You could tell that sometimes the coach was like "Damn, we are going up against a D-I school" or maybe they were thinking, "I don't know if this kid is good enough to play at that level." Coach Harold at Drury was different, though. He was very confident in his program and felt that he could offer what I was looking for. Early on in our conversations, I was straightforward from the beginning that it was my desire to play Division I if the opportunity presented itself.

Again, my Mom, Dad, Coach Ireland, and I hopped in the car on a September school day and we were off to visit Drury. As soon as we found the campus, we pulled right up to a spot that had a sign printed: "Reserved for Morgan Eye." I was already impressed by their subtle but very thoughtful hospitality. We toured the gym and the locker room. The locker room had just been re-done and they had new lockers made with dark cherry wood. All costs for the locker-room update were provided by donors to the team. The coaches talked a lot about the amazing fan support that they had there in Springfield. They told stories of the little old ladies that would even try to feed the girls cookies during pregame warmups—I think the coaches probably made them wait until after. They also had to name-drop Brad Pitt by explaining how his mother came to every home game and was a huge supporter of the team. I was very impressed by that, to be honest, and thought it was pretty cool.

I remember the bulk of my conversations being with Coach Harold and assistant coach Shelly Jones. My parents, Coach Ireland, and I followed Coach Harold and Coach Jones to a quiet area and they laid out what Drury was all about. I remember Coach Jones setting a very large book on the table in front of us. Referring to the book as she gently tapped it, "This is what we are all about. There are some coffee stains, makeup stains, maybe even hair-spray on this thing, but that's because it's real." She went on to say that she was going to describe everything that their program was about first. They did not want me to tell them what I was looking for and then in turn have them respond with what they could offer. She wanted to lay it all out from the get-go first so as not to think they were conforming to my needs.

That had a lasting impression on me. I loved how her book looked like it had been through it all, I loved that they were not going to try to sugarcoat anything. Both coaches talked a lot about how hard their team played. They were ranked nationally in Division II, they were well known for their tough-nosed defense, and they had a great fan base. They promised me that I would be pushed every day to be the best I could be. Coach Harold proceeded to say, "I am offering you a full-ride scholar-ship. I want to hand the keys to you as a freshman and I want you to be our point guard." That was a very bold statement and this man had never even watched me play in person. I was, honestly, a little shocked, but also over-whelmed with confidence that he thought I could come in and be a difference-maker.

The last thing we did was tour the gym, which was a very nice Division II facility. It had red seats, great light-ing, and the floor had a nice clean finish on it. We were just standing around and then Coach Jones encouraged me to go take a shot. I may have taken my jacket off for this one. I dribbled the ball down to the far side of the court from where my family and the coaches stood be-hind. I went to the left elbow area, about a 17-foot shot, just slightly in front of the three-point line because, let's be honest, I was super stiff and was afraid I wouldn't get it there. I narrowed my eyes on my target and let that sucker fly … and hit nothing but net. The coaches kept saying how I looked at home on their court. I joked with them before leaving, "Hey I am 100 percent on this court." On the ride home, Coach Ireland was like, "That was a big shot. Getting up, not having warmed up, and knowing everyone was watching you." Before I even played a college game, I think I had a knack for knocking down big shots.

On the ride home, I was sitting in the back with Coach Ireland and he asked me my thoughts on the visit. I had nothing but good things to say. He could tell that I had an uneasy feeling. He said, "You didn't think you were going to like it that much, did you?" He was absolutely right. I thought for sure I would go there and be unimpressed and my decision would be super easy. But there were definitely a lot of intriguing things about the visit. I had yet to receive an offer from Mizzou, so that gave me a lot of uncertainty.

As my senior year finally approached, I was beginning to feel a little uneasy about my collegiate future. I just really wanted to have everything decided before I got too far into my senior basketball season. I wanted my full focus to be on my senior season. It would be ideal for me to get signed in the early signing period in November of 2010.

I already knew Drury wanted me. Coach Harold had offered me a full ride and the keys to running the team without having even watched me play in person. However, I still did not know exactly how Mizzou felt about me. So one day I had to build up the courage to call Coach Pingeton and see where we were at. I had to leave a message, because it was not unusual that we played phone tag before we could catch one another. I left her a message about my visit with Drury and that they had offered. I just wanted to know where they stood and how soon I would be able to know if they were interested in offering or not.

I remember her calling me back just as I pulled up to my house after school one day. I sat in my little S10 pick-up truck, my heart racing, and palms sweaty (as usual), and I answered my phone. Our conversation went great. Coach P strongly encouraged me not to make any big decisions just yet. I assured her that I had no intention of committing to Drury without finding out more from Mizzou.

Coach P explained that she really wanted to see me play in person. She felt she needed to see a player with her own two eyes before offering a scholarship. It's funny now, because that was the total opposite of Coach Harold. However, I really respected Coach P's outlook and reasoning. We finally found a date that was good for Coach P to be able to make it to a game. It would be after the early signing period was over, but I was still hopeful to have a decision made by Christmas as to where I would continue my basketball career.

Chapter

No one could miss the bright gold Mizzou sweat-shirt Coach P was wearing as she entered the small gymnasium at Montrose High School.  She arrived early to the game and sat in the soon-to-be filled bleachers as parents and adults in the community were all still getting off work. Our team was warming up on the far end. My teammate Felicia rushed over as soon as she saw Coach Pingeton. She put a basketball up to her mouth so as to disguise what she was saying and whispered out the side of her mouth, "Coach P has entered the building."

I saw her enter the gym — our gym isn't that big. I remember feeling calm, for the most part. I think knowing she was there, I just wanted to prove what I could do. It felt like I was sinking every shot during warmups. I was ready to go. I saw my parents arrive and they sat on the same side as Coach P, but down closer to the end where we were warming up on. I noticed my high school coach walk over to speak with Coach P. After he chatted with her for a second, I saw him go directly to my parents. I found out later that Coach P wanted my parents to know that she wasn't able to say hello to them or talk to them because of NCAA compliance rules (Compliance rules are the devil's work. I don't know who comes up with some of the silly rules). But I thought, wow, that was a really nice gesture from Coach P to do that.

We played Osceola that evening, the alma mater of Jordan Garrison, whom I referenced earlier as another small-school native looking to play Division I. She had just graduated and was in her first year at Creighton Uni-

versity in Omaha, Nebraska. I couldn't tell you how much
I scored that game or how well I played, but I remember
getting into foul trouble early in the first half and having
to sit for what felt like a large part of the game. I remember my coach pleading with the official about the calls,
knowing that Coach P had come all that way to watch me.

We got way ahead and took the game to a running
clock in the second half, so our freshman came out to get
minutes in the fourth quarter. That was a good thing, to
have a big lead and have had a solid game. It wasn't great
for Coach Jones from Drury, who came from Springfield
that night but got caught coming the wrong way because
of highway construction, which caused her to miss the entire first half. So picture that. Montrose High School's tiny
gymnasium packed with Bluejays fans, one bright gold
Mizzou sweatshirt in the sea of blue, and a black and red
Drury jacket sitting directly across the gym from Coach
Pingeton in the front row.

I had no idea that Drury was going to make the game
that evening. I was flattered to have not only one coach
recruiting me, but two who made it to my hometown to
see me play. That's a really cool thing that I think kids forget about. These coaches have families and they are taking
time away from them and their team to travel to see you
play because they think you may have what it takes to
help their program.

I got home from the game that night a little after 9
p.m. after watching our boys team play. I quickly showered and then had to study for a Spanish quiz the next
day. I was sitting on the floor in my room with my Spanish book open and notes and work pages spread out as
I quizzed myself.  Then I heard my phone start buzzing
on the floor. I looked down to see who it was, and it was
Coach Pingeton. I didn't have too much time to let myself
get nervous this time because I had to answer it.  Coach

P said she had just gotten back to Mizzou Arena and she was parked in the parking lot (she still remembers this to this day).

I told her I was just working on some Spanish homework. We rehashed the game and she told me what she saw and thought. She said she noticed during warmups how I was sinking every shot even knowing she was there. I didn't seem to get tense or nervous. She described it as "ice in my veins" and she could see me making big-time shots for her team in the future. So far, I liked how this conversation was going.

She said even with the bad calls, she admired the minimal reactions that I had to the officials and how I handled myself. She said she couldn't really evaluate my defense too much because I was sitting for much of the time with foul trouble and we were forced into playing more zone defense than usual.

She wrapped up the conversation by asking me to be a Mizzou Tiger. I honestly can't tell you what I exactly responded with, but she ended up saying, "You don't have to say anything or decide anything right now if you want to sleep on it and talk with your parents." I calmly said that yes, I wanted to give it a couple days. It took everything I had not to scream, "HELL YES, WHERE DO I SIGN?"

Three days had passed and my parents and I were new to this recruiting thing, so we thought we had a little more time before we needed to respond to Mizzou. But Coach P called my high school coach — another compliance rule, so she couldn't call me — to make sure that I was still interested. I remember we were getting ready for practice and Coach Ireland was on his phone and he called me over to ask me, "You are leaning toward Mizzou, right?" I knew deep down that I wanted to go there. I think I just gave it time to make sure everything sunk

in and that Drury was not what I wanted. The next day
I called Coach P and I said, "I would love to be a Tiger."
That was all she wrote. My dream of becoming a Division
I basketball player was coming true.

The phone call to Coach P was one of the highlights
of my senior year. The bad part was making the other call
to the coach you are turning down. Shortly after my high
of telling Coach P that I wanted to be a Tiger, I had to flip
the switch and call Coach Harold from Drury. The one
thing that made the call less hurtful was knowing that I
told him from the beginning that my desire was to play
Division I, if given the opportunity. It was still difficult,
but I thanked Coach Harold for everything he had done
for me and the hospitality they all showed toward me and
my family.

# 15

Chapter

**N**ow that I knew where I was going to attend college, I could completely shift my focus to enjoying my last year of high school basketball. It was a memorable year, to say the least. On my senior night, I broke my childhood idol Tina McClain's career scoring record by scoring 2,367 points. Immediately after I hit the layup to break the record, the whistle blew really fast and I was confused as to what was going on. Was there a foul? Had I traveled? As I looked around, I saw Coach Ireland had called a timeout instantly after I scored the basket and just behind him and our bench was a sign that read, "Congrats Morgan, 2,367+ points."

All my teammates huddled around me and we embraced in a big hug. I love those girls so much and they are a part of that record. That win on senior night also gave my fellow seniors and I our 100th career win. It was quite the way to finish my career in a gym that was home for so many years — from a little girl playing in third grade hitting game-winning shots to a senior in high school leaving her legacy.

Our team easily won our district tournament and cruised past our opponent in the sectional game, so only one game stood in our way to advancing to the final four for the second year in a row. It was a game that had a lot of hype built up around it. We would be facing Walnut Grove and a lot of people thought that they were going to beat us. I think our team really got fired up when we would read what other people were saying and how we heard that we were going to lose. They fueled the fire for sure. That game, I didn't score well, to say the least. What made that game so special was that you saw that our team was a great TEAM! I didn't need to do all of the scoring. Everyone played their role and we ended up having a running clock in the fourth quarter en route to our victory to take us to back to Columbia for another final four.

I have to be honest. I am 26 years old now, and writing about this next part of my story is still uncomfortable and a little painful. Our team faced Marion County in the semifinal game at Mizzou Arena. We were the better team, and I'll argue that until I die. Again, the game is mostly a blur to me. I got in foul trouble and, of course, I remember them being very bad and tough calls. We had the lead in the fourth quarter with only seconds remaining. Marion County's point guard dribbled down the

When I broke the school scoring record at Montrose, my coach called timeout and all my teammates joined me to celebrate. It was special.

78

court, and all we needed to do was slow her down. She got to the right baseline and sunk the shot to give them the lead. I called timeout, all of us stunned. We didn't really have time to get off any kind of quality shot. Just like that, it was over. We were not going to repeat as state champs. None of us knew how to react, because we hadn't lost a game since our sophomore season. Tears came rushing immediately. It was the most awful feeling I have ever felt. I had let down my team, my school, my community.

Our fans and family didn't know what to do either, because they were used to seeing us win. We met our families on the concourse, where they were waiting there to console us. I think they needed just as much consoling as we did. The tears came even harder after seeing everyone, and I felt the guilt even more. As I hugged people, the only thing I could say was, "I'm sorry." I genuinely felt like it was my fault because I was going to make sure that we won state again. Looking back now as an older adult, I put so much pressure on myself. And as much as it still pains me to think of that game because I know we were the better team, I think we all learned a lot of valuable lessons that day.

That night our team went out to dinner at a Chinese buffet. I sat near Coach Ireland. He kept pinching his nose with his thumb and index finger into the corner of his eyes. I found out later from his wife that he was keeping tears from streaming down his face. I know he felt just as bad as we did.

After we finished our food, Coach Ireland opened his fortune cookie. He read it, gave a quick smirk and showed me the fortune. The fortune read: "Time heals all wounds." Usually when things like that happen, all I can do is smile and say, "Good one, God."

That night at the hotel, the emotions got the best of

me yet again. Felicia was my roommate and she did her best to console me because I was sobbing uncontrollably at that point. I don't know that I got much sleep that night, but either way we had to regroup and play the next day in the third-place game. I got some of the best advice I could have gotten to re-shift my thinking and finish my career the right way. Coach Hankins spoke with me in the hotel lobby. He told me, "People have seen what you girls can do when you win. You don't have to end your season on a loss. You get one more game. Now you get to show them what you can do after a loss." He was right. Of course we wanted to be playing our last game together for the state title, but that wasn't going to happen now. But we did get one more game together, and we won the third-place game easily. I finished with more than 100 wins in my high school career, and after that last game, I had 2,537 career points at Montrose, a school record that still stands.

All of those years of playing with my best friends were now over. We spent countless Saturday mornings practicing, with our parents watching from the bleachers. We shared memories of limo rides to our games, sleepovers in the hotel rooms, and dominating teams who gave us one look and thought we were a bunch of scrubs. I was blessed beyond belief. I got to play with my best friends growing up and I think it really allowed me to showcase my skills because we were such a close-knit team and it helped develop me as a leader.

I honestly don't know how I would have done on a traveling team where I wouldn't know quite what my role was or didn't quite know my teammates either. I got the best of both worlds. I played with my girls growing up and I still got an opportunity to play at a big-time school in college.

# 16
## Chapter

**F**reshman year was probably my most challenging time in college, which probably wasn't all that unusual. It was a year full of transition. I was going off to college to live on my own for the first time in my life, at a place that was a hundred times bigger than my hometown. I would be responsible for doing my own laundry, getting food, waking up on my own, going to class, etc. The biggest transition, of course, was playing Division I basketball. It was a challenging year, but it was also my biggest year of personal growth. I learned a ton about myself and started to grow as a woman. You learn so much that first year, even though it was overwhelming at times.

I remember the first day I met Kyley Simmons, Bree Fowler, and JUCO transfer Liz Smith. Together Kyley, Bree, and myself would make up the freshman class and the first recruiting class of Coach P's tenure at Mizzou. We left my home early in the morning to make the two-hour drive and hopefully avoid some of the chaos of all of the incoming freshman headed off to college at the same time. I drove my own vehicle very closely behind my mom because I still had no idea where we were driving to. I got a bit nervous driving in "bigger cities." We made it to the Defoe Graham dorms, my home for the summer session. We pulled up into the temporary unloading parking zone, got checked in and started unloading.

The first teammate I met was Kyley Simmons. Kyley is probably one of the most fun, outgoing, crazy girls I have ever met. She definitely helped me come out of my shell. If it wasn't for her, I would not have met as many people as I did. We hit it off right away and I felt comfortable around her.

Then I met Bree Fowler. I have so many great things to say about this girl that I could probably write a separate book on her alone. Bree was the one who gave me my nickname "Mo." It was a random day when Bree said, "I think I have a nickname for you. What about Mo?" I liked it and it stuck. I recall being in the middle of an individual workout and Bree hollered out, "You got it, Mo!" Coach Putnam heard Bree and said, "Can I call you Mo?" I liked the nickname because I never really had one growing up. Bree and I became best friends over the years. We literally went through everything together. We were an unlikely friendship that flourished and we always pick up right where we left off every time we see one another.

Together, Kyley was the crazy outgoing one, Bree was very laid-back, calm and cool, and I landed somewhere in the middle. We balanced one another perfectly. We were a fun trio. I remember times just laughing about literally nothing. We had a lot of fun times together in the dorms and got to know a lot of the other athletes as well.

My first roommate was junior college transfer Liz Smith. I won't lie, I was a little intimated to room with someone who was not also a freshman. She had already experienced two years of college and here I come, as a little eighteen-year-old girl. But I could not have asked for a better roommate. I only got to room with Liz for the summer session, but I loved every second of it. To me, Liz was always very wise. I listened every time she offered advice. And dang, that girl is funny. I picked up a lot of one-liners from her, too. She was one of my many teammates who I learned loved to watch SpongeBob while taking a mid-day nap. But how could I judge when I always took in a dose of That 70's Show and Friends.

Like I mentioned, freshman year is very overwhelming. You have a ton of new stuff thrown at you and, luckily, I got really good at time management. You have to if you want to get good grades, excel on the court, somewhat keep a sane mindset and enjoy what you are doing. A typical day for me would be an early morning class, get my shots in (usually 200-500 makes, typically on the shooting gun), eat lunch, head to my afternoon classes, back to arena for practice, then weights, then probably a cold tub, dinner, homework … and repeat.

Sprinkle in some mandatory speaking sessions we had to attend in the evenings and you've got yourself a full and busy day. I will say something that you must do, and I think a lot of other former athletes will say this, but it is important to allow yourself YOU time. I recall one senior athlete speaking at a Women 4 Women meeting and she said she always let herself watch her favorite show on whatever the night of the week it was. That was something I always did with Bree Fowler. Early on, it was Grey's Anatomy, and we always watched that together every Thursday night. Our senior year, it was How to Get Away With Murder. I just thought it was really good insight from that girl to tell the younger athletes that you need that time for yourself. Whether it be to read, write, go to the movies or get ice cream, it's okay to give yourself that treat.

\*\*\*   \*\*\*   \*\*\*

**O**ne of my biggest mistakes as a freshman was self-comparison. I did this in many areas of my life at the time, first with the weight room. I'll be honest, I may have lifted weights here and there throughout high school, but it was never something that I did consistently or had much knowledge about. Luckily, in preparation for coming to Mizzou, my coaches sent workouts on a DVD to

explain the different movements. Once my high school
senior season was over, I started on that. I could not do
a pull-up to save my life, let alone an eccentric pull-up.
What does eccentric even mean? I did my pull-ups in
our Montrose locker room on the bar that was our coat
hanger. You have to get creative when you're from a
small school and a weight room isn't in the budget. Since
I couldn't do a pull-up, I had to jump to start and then
slowly lower myself (eccentric) for the time it said. At
first, I did not even come close to making the times. My
arms just could not hold my body. They would start to
burn and I wouldn't be able to hold myself up for the entire time. Slowly but surely, I did make the times, though,
and I felt a small victory in seeing some progress. Pull-ups
would only come to haunt me further when I made it to
campus.

I remember shortly after beginning the workouts
in high school that our assistant coach, Coach Hankins,
told me I should probably add some cardio after I lift. I
remember thinking to myself "Yeah right. I'm dead tired
after I lift. No way I could go run a few miles." It's funny I
thought that, because I would be pushed way harder once
I made it to campus at Mizzou. I thought I worked hard
in high school, but it didn't come close to the work I was
about to put in during my four years in college.

I kept up with the weightlifting until it was time to
head off for the summer session at Mizzou. The coaches wanted us somewhat prepared when we arrived, so
I made sure to always get my lifting in. I held myself
accountable even though it would have been easy to tell
my coaches that I worked out on my own, even if I hadn't.
What good would that do for anyone, though? I would be
cheating myself and cheating my teammates had I done
that.

When I arrived for summer session, we were introduced to our new strength and conditioning coach. He was different from the guy who had sent the workout DVD. I wasn't sure what to think of someone new coming in, but I can now say it was the best thing to ever happen to me, and our entire women's basketball program. Coach Jacob Linn really believed in me and knew that I had what it took to make the changes I needed to transform my body so I could perform at my best. Coach Linn is so sweet. Talk about a guy who brings a great attitude to work every single day. That positivity was contagious and I think he looked at it that way, too. He often had to work with us girls at the wee hours in the morning, grumpy, tired, and not looking forward whatsoever to some type of stupid conditioning that would leave us exhausted. He took a different approach. It was an opportunity for us to get better.

With the weights, Coach Linn monitored our progress in just about every area. Each year he improved the way he monitored things and charted our progress. I always saw him constantly researching, reading, and learning ways to improve the body. Just as with anything, you have to begin somewhere, so we all had our baseline numbers. All of our numbers would be tracked and it was compared to the ideal number we wanted to achieve. On our own charts, you would have the activity that was re-corded and when you reached that ideal number, the box was filled in with yellow — meaning you had reached the "standard" for that particular category.

Let's just say for a long time, my sheet had no yellow boxes on it. It was somewhat depressing and demoraliz-ing to see other girls began with yellow boxes, or quickly earning them, and I had none. There were girls on my team who were the same weight as me or even smaller, and they were lifting more than me. How could that be possible? I felt very insecure about that and couldn't understand why I couldn't lift just as much as them.

*** *** ***

The second mistake I made in self-comparison was body composition. A lot of Division I athletes have probably heard of the dreaded DXA machine, which feels like a violation of your body. It reads your body fat composition and tells your nutritionist what parts of your body have either gained or lost fat and muscle.

Again, there was a "standard" or "ideal" number of body fat composition we wanted to achieve. The number I was told at the time for a female athlete was anywhere between 18 and 22 percent body fat. I had no idea where I would fall on the chart. I felt like I was in decent shape, by no means fat or anything. My first DXA revealed I was far from the standard. I came in at 32 percent body fat, which by the standard would actually consider me obese. That was silly.

Still, I won't lie, I was quite embarrassed by that number because I was an athlete and I felt there was no way that I should be that high. Coach P talked to some of us about our numbers and I told her mine was higher than I thought it would be and she just responded with, "Not a big deal, but just something good to be aware of." That actually made me feel a lot better.

*** *** ***

The third and final mistake of comparison I made was on the basketball court. I can't even begin to explain the difference in the transition from high school basketball to college. The game is so much faster and more physical. The level of competition is ridiculous compared to high school. Everyone on your team was probably the "star" on their high school team and now all of the "stars" are on the same team.  During the summer of my freshman year, we played a lot of pick-up games of five-on-five throughout the week. There were some days that I did just fine or even felt a glimmer of greatness. Other days, I thought there was no way I had any business being out there on the court.

The buildup of self-comparison in the weight room, nutritionally, and on the court weighed heavily on me. We had started official practices, and they took their toll on me as well. I got to where I was in class literally counting down the dreaded hours and minutes before I had to go to practice. As the time approached, my anxiety would only rise. At practice, I felt like I could not do one single thing right. We would move from drill to drill so fast and there was so much terminology that I just did not understand yet. I would get so consumed and focused on trying not to mess up that I would mess up anyway and then also get yelled at for not opening my mouth and talking.

My mind was always in a rush and my heart would start pounding uncontrollably when my name was singled out. When a whistle would blow to stop play, and I would hear "Mo," I would instantly think, "crap." The first time I made a mistake, Coach P blew the whistle and said, "Mo, deep four." I ran to the baseline and started running on the side of the court to stay out of the way. Only problem was I had no idea what the hell a 'deep four' was.

As I ran by Coach Putnam, I whispered, "What's a deep four?" She told me it was just down and back twice. I could have been running for a long time had I not asked. I can laugh about those moments now. I laugh even more when Bree Fowler shared a story at our senior banquet. She wrote something along the lines of: "Mo would be on the side (of the court) running and I'm thinking to myself,

"Uh, Coach, you sure about her?" I think at the time Bree was kind of wondering why I was recruited to play at Mizzou, and guess what, I had the same thoughts. Today it's fun to joke about how much Coach P was always on me, and with good reason. It definitely made me a better player in the long run.

# 17
Chapter

**I had the opportunity** to go home one more time before our games started. As a freshman, we were told by the upperclassmen to always check in with Coach P before leaving town just to make sure nothing was going on. I poked my head into Coach P's office and asked if it would be alright if I headed home for the weekend. I would like to think I have a pretty good game face or put up a good front, but Coach P saw right through it. (She always has). She asked me if everything was alright, and I said yes. She asked if I was sure, because she could sense some sadness in my voice. She asked me to close the door and then I sat down in a chair on the opposite side of her desk—and broke down and cried.

I let it all out. I told Coach P that I felt I wasn't as good as my teammates, or as fast or athletic. I had a lot of doubt over whether I could play at this level. She asked me if there was anyone on the team who could shoot better than me. I threw out some names, but she said no, that I was the best shooter. She said, "Mo, we recruited you for a reason. We didn't make a mistake."

She started making me realize my value to the team. Coach P then encouraged me to go home that weekend, get out my high school scrapbooks, and look at all that I had achieved. It would be a reminder for me that I was a good basketball player and I could play at this level.

Coach P and I still talk about that meeting to this day. We joke about how far I came from the freshman in tears who thought she couldn't make it at this level. We proved that little freshman wrong.

89

*** *** ***

I **headed home to** Montrose for the weekend, and I did as Coach P had said and looked back at my high school scrapbooks. Although it somewhat boosted my confidence, I still honestly didn't enjoy one single day at

My coach at Missouri, Robin Pingeton, could always tell when something was bothering me. She defintely got the best out of me.

home because the entire time all I could think about was how I had to go back to Columbia. I didn't want to go back to classes, workouts, practices, and weights. I just wanted to be at home. My family quickly picked up on my mood and could sense something was wrong with me.

My sister Lauren and I love taking a Sunday cruise with our dog, Copper, in the back of the truck. We'd stop to grab a soda and some peanut M&M's. Since I wasn't acting myself, I think my mom encouraged my sister to take me for our Sunday ride. Again, I had my emotional breakdown. I confided in my sister about how I didn't want to let anyone down. I felt that I couldn't play at this level. I wasn't as fast, strong, or athletic as any of the other girls. I just didn't want to not reach my communities' expectations, my old/new coaches' expectations, and my own expectations. My sister got a little emotional having seen how upset I was and she just told me, "Morgan, everyone is so proud of you already. It doesn't even matter what you do. Whether you get to play or not, everyone is already so proud."

It was just what I needed. Letting out my emotions to both Coach P and my sister lifted so much weight off of my shoulders. I didn't always have to be the "suffer-in-silent" type, which I find out again later. I reluctantly headed back to Columbia. I remember my sister telling me about her experiences in college and how, "sometimes, you will have days that you cry, but when you look back later, you kind of laugh at yourself and wonder why you were crying in the first place." She was absolutely right about that one. A few days after returning to school, my sister sent me a text that has served as one of my favorite quotes all through college and to this day. "One day at a time — this is enough. Do not look back and grieve over the past, for it is gone; and do not be troubled about the future for it has not yet come. Live in the present, and make it so beautiful that it will be worth remembering" — Ida Scott Taylor.

It was like a flip of a switch. I still had my moments of doubt, of weakness, and of feeling sorry for myself. Now it was time to take it "one day at a time." It was easy to be reminded of as Coach P would tell us before the break of each huddle to "get better TODAY!" I started gaining confidence by the day, and accepted that it wasn't going to happen overnight. I knew I just had to try to get a little bit better each day.

I recall one day having a pretty rough practice and I was on the verge of tears. We were all spread out around the court, stretching with IT bands. I flipped on my side with the purple band wrapped around my foot, pulling the band above my shoulder to stretch my quad. As I laid there, replaying how awful I had played, Coach Michael Porter came by and simply said, "Dude, be patient with yourself. You're going to do special things here."

Patient. It seems like a simple word with simple meaning, but it is such a hated word because of what it asks of you. It tells you that you cannot have immediate gratification. You have to put in the time and put in the work. He was right, though. Just like Coach P and my sister were right — one day at a time. Be patient. It is fun to look back today and think how awesome it was that Coach Porter saw greatness in me. He saw something in that little freshman who struggled early on, who came from a town no one had heard of, who received only one Division I offer. That little freshman had a dream — he saw it, and he played a part in pulling it out.

Once I stopped comparing myself to others and focused on doing my best, that was when I turned the corner. Like I said, it really took tremendous focus to be in the PRESENT. There were a lot of factors that play into that mentality that I will get into later on. Stopping the self-comparison, I started seeing results in the weight room. I was getting personal records. Every time a team-mate achieved a personal record, Coach Linn shouted, "PR! MORGAN EYE!" and all of your teammates cheered and came to give you a high-five. I didn't care if I wasn't squatting or benching as much as my fellow teammates. I only cared that I showed improvement from the last time I performed that exercise. I can proudly say that by the time I graduated as a senior, I had a whole lot more yellow boxes.

My senior year, we got tested on pull-ups. My great-est fear had come back around full circle. We had to try to do as many non-assisted pull-ups as we could and we had to lift our chin beyond a certain mark for it to count. It wasn't common during weights to have to do non-assist-ed pull-ups (mostly because I couldn't do them). Usually we did band-assisted pull-ups or eccentric, in which I could jump my way to the top and slowly lower my body. This time however, it was all on me—no assistance. We had a normal workout that day and, as you made your way through the workout, we all took our turn at being tested at the pull-ups. As I began my workout, I started to feel a lot of anxiety. I thought I was back in my high school locker room on the coat rack struggling to hold my weight, or my freshman year when I struggled so badly to perform the number of pull-ups on our workout list. I approached Coach Linn at the pull-up station. My heart was pounding, my body felt like it had chills. I stepped up on the life-fitness machine and decided to start above the chin-up mark, lower down and then pull up. I jumped up, lowered and, to my surprise, lifted my chin above the band for one rep. Holy smokes! I went for another. I began to kick my legs .... just one more. I got it! Now this may sound pathetic to some people, but I could not be more proud of being able to perform two pull-ups all on my own. The anxiety I felt before was more real than I ever could have imagined. It was something that I feared doing because I feared failing—and I feared failing in front of others. That day I faced my fear, and all of my continued hard work showed off that day.

*** *** ***

**M**y self-comparison on the DXA numbers simply came down to understanding that we are all built different and I need to love and accept my body. I knew I could improve my eating habits — no doubt about that at all. I was what you would call a "simple-but-picky eater." I basically had the palate of an eight-year-old. I just wanted a cheeseburger—and hold all those veggie toppings. The first time I had a salad was at my senior prom, and that was only because I knew I would be heading off to college for basketball and needed to get used to eating healthier. Basically, the types of fruit I would eat were apples and bananas. I would eat some canned fruit like peaches or pears, but when it came to raw fruits, bananas and apples were the only ones I liked. Vegetables included corn, green beans, potatoes, canned carrots (they had to be from a can or forget about it). I have since learned that canned food does not have as many nutrients as the raw kinds.

As I became more and more knowledgeable about food, I made wiser decisions. I also just started trying more and more foods. The Mizzou Athletic Training Complex (MATC) offered fresh fruit every day (something I really took for granted was to have fresh fruit cut up for me every day—my mom and sister always were envious of that). Today I eat just about anything. I love ALL fruits. Like how was it possible that I didn't enjoy strawberries, blueberries, raspberries, pineapple, honeydew, cantaloupe, watermelon, and so much more? Oh, how I love vegetables! I will eat a salad all the time now. I will also eat raw vegetables, but I do enjoy them the most when they are cooked or in a stir-fry.

It's funny to talk to my mom and sister, who can't believe how I completely changed my taste buds — or at least exposed my taste buds to new things. They are also surprised I can cook. I remember before heading off to college that they were a little concerned about my survival. Okay, I am being dramatic as far as survival, but I think they still had concerns and rightfully so. I really didn't do much cooking when I lived at home. But that was my exact plan. I always tell them, "Why would I cook when you two already do it?" My mom and sister are great cooks and it would have been wrong to deprive them of that special talent — I was just the taste-tester. When Mom would cook for events, I can still see my Dad and I hovering in the kitchen hoping she "botched" something so we could have it for ourselves.

I cook a lot now and I try to make things as healthy as I can. I love making egg-white omelets filled with peppers, onions, tomatoes and meat. I love making stir fry packed full of veggies. My new-found love is making zoodles — noodles made from zucchini. I also like to make spaghetti using spaghetti squash. I still eat "basic foods," but I try to put healthy spins on them. For instance, making a pizza, I use a flatbread wrap and then use avocado for my sauce, add some meat, veggies, and a little cheese. I won't go further since this isn't a cookbook. However, it was another way that basketball impacted my life. I knew I needed to fuel my body with the right things to be able to perform at my peak day in and day out. This even meant when I went home on breaks, I couldn't just let myself completely go. I definitely let myself have treats while at home, but I had to make sure I was smart about how I did it. At the end of the day, I always thought about my team before I made decisions. What I fueled my body with would impact my performance and ultimately the team as well.

*** *** ***

**M**y first DXA in the fall of my first year, I was measured at 31.5 percent body fat. By the end of my first year of playing, I got it all the way down to 26.9 percent. I remember getting the results and Coach Linn was ecstatic. He hollered to me in the weight room, "What the heck did you do?" I told him I've just been eating better and it helped that it was Lent because I usually give up sweets. All it took was for me to make some changes in my life and I felt amazing. I focused one day at a time and my result was so sweet! I was not done, though. I still wanted to get my percentage into the standard zone and I knew I still had room for improvement. I also want to acknowledge that we should never fixate ourselves on the numbers, whether that be a body-comp number or the number on the scale. It truly comes down to how you feel as a person and that you love yourself. I know there have been a lot of people, athletes specifically, who become fixated on hitting a certain number and they go to unhealthy lengths to achieve those things. It is hard because of the society we live in which values looks so much. But that is when you have to forget what others think and know that you are truly loved by God and you should love your body just as God loves you. I think loving your body means doing your absolute best to feed it the "right stuff" that means physically, emotionally, psychologically, and spiritually.

This topic actually reminds me of a Cherokee tale that Coach Porter shared with our team during our chapel after one of our pregame meals. The story was about a Cherokee Indian tribe. The grandfather was telling a story to his grandson about two wolves—one good, one evil. We all have a good wolf and an evil wolf that lives inside of us. Eventually the two wolves fight. The grandson asked his grandfather, "Which wolf wins?" The wise grandfather replies, "The one you feed." Let that sink in for a second. If you fill yourself with evil—negative thoughts, self-pity, envy, etc.—the evil wolf wins. If you fill yourself with good—positive thoughts, hope, faith, love, etc.—the good wolf wins. This story can be used in many ways in how we go about feeding the "good" or "evil" wolf inside of us. Whenever I find myself feeling sorry for myself, I am feeding the bad wolf and, believe me, we are all human and have those times of weakness.

However, you have to be sure to feed the good wolf even more; that way he will win. So the next time you feel yourself wallowing in self-pity, ask yourself when the last time was that you fed the good wolf.

# 18
Chapter

**I had a friend tell me** how excited she was to come watch my games during my first year. That feeling made me a little uneasy because I didn't know what playing time would look like. I gave her a warning, "I don't even know how much I'll play. I'm on the black squad right now."

Black squad basically meant that at practice I reversed my jersey to black while the starters and the first two subs were all in gold. I wanted to be honest with her and realistic that I may not see as much playing time as we all might hope for. It all came back to me not wanting to disappoint anyone, including myself, if I didn't reach expectations.

I was finally finding my groove at practice, but it was not always easy. I had definitely come along since my talk with Coach P about looking at my scrapbooks and riding around with my sister. Even though I was building confidence by the day, that didn't mean I didn't have my bad days, and my days where doubt would try to creep in.

I started to get a little more playing time with the starting five, so during practice Coach P would have me switch my jersey over to gold from time to time to get reps. We were in a five-on-five drill and she had me switch over to gold to get some reps at the point guard position. I did as I was told and jumped right in. After a few times going up and down the court, our starting point guard Kyley asked to sub in for me, so I headed to the sideline and waited to sub back in for the gold team. As I'm watching my teammates from the sideline, all of a

99

sudden I hear Coach P's voice. She looks over at me and questions me, saying, "Is the black team just not going to have a point guard, Mo?" I was really confused because I was wearing a gold jersey because she had told me about two possessions prior to switch over to gold. So what was I missing here? I quickly took off my jersey and flipped it inside out to go back on the black team.

As the action finally came to a stop and I was able to sub in, Coach P continues in my ear. "You just taking the day off? I don't know how they do things in Montrose, but we don't take days off here." Damn, that at was one of the biggest blows I ever got. I instantly got so angry. When I talk about being prideful from where I come from, I mean it. I was so fired up after she made that comment. It's quite funny looking back on the memory now because I know she was just trying to get my riled up … and it worked!

\*\*\*   \*\*\*   \*\*\*

**W**hat is sort of neat about this story is that a couple years later when I was a junior, I had the opportunity to really be a leader for one of our incoming freshmen. Sierra Michaelis was a small-town girl just like myself. We often joke to this day of who comes from a smaller town. My town has a population of 384 and her town of Mercer, Missouri is just slightly smaller. However, I graduated in a class of 12 (including our foreign exchange student, Sylvain) and her class was a whopping 14!

There was no question we could relate to one another in a lot of ways. An occasion arose during a practice when Coach P jumped all over Sierra for making a soft turnover. Coach P darted at Sierra, "This isn't 1A anymore. You can't be soft." I wish I could watch video footage to see what my exact reaction was. All I know was I watched

Sierra closely to see how she would take those words because I knew, two years prior, those exact words stung me real good. I made sure to reach out to Sierra after practice to see how she was. We both are prideful of our little hometowns and don't take a liking to any bad-mouthing about where we were from. I told her about my almost exact situation my freshman year and understood that it probably stung, but also told her to realize Coach P was just lighting a fire under her. Sierra went on to have a heck of a career at Mizzou. I enjoyed getting to play with my other half of the "1A Wonders" — self-proclaimed and named. Any time I held up a '1' sign with my finger, Sierra always threw back an 'A' with two fingers.

During my second year as a graduate assistant at Missouri — yes, I know I'm getting ahead of myself, but this is an important story — I saw one of our players get challenged by Coach P during a game and it made me think back to all of the times when she really got at me and challenged me. I saw the player and her reaction, and she was not handling it well.

I remember being in that situation where it just cut you deep to your core and emotionally you could not handle it as best as you wanted to. I thought back to my freshman season. We had just finished our last game of the non-conference and got to head home for a short Christmas break. I finally started to gain confidence in my play, with my team, and competing at the Division I level. However, the last team we played before break was very athletic. I recall beating the team relatively easily, but I remember that I didn't have my best game. At a time when I felt I was gaining momentum, it stunk going home on break feeling that I had taken a few steps back. I drove home that night after the game with my sister. It was so sweet to be home. The very next day I got a call from Coach P while I was at home. She called just to check in on me, because she could sense something just wasn't quite right with me. I am more of a suffer-in-silence type of person, which has not been good for me, as I found out during my time as a G.A. I remember her encouraging me and telling me that the team we had just played was the most athletic team we had faced thus far. As a young freshman, I had not yet learned how to combat others' athleticism with my basketball smarts. Coach P went on to explain to me that she just wanted to make sure I was doing alright and that it was not like she was going up and down the roster calling everyone, but sensed that she needed to reach out to me. It seriously amazes me the power that Coach P has. There is something about every conversation I have with her, I feel better about myself, the situation, and our relationship.

*** *** ***

By the time our games started, I found myself gaining confidence each game and had a few breakout moments. We traveled to Texas for a two-game swing to open the season. In our first game, Kyley Simmons, who was our only point guard, got in foul trouble early. As I watched Kyley pick up another foul, I knew what was about to happen. Coach P called my name, and I went in for Kyley. Point guard was not my true position, but I had to step in from time to time for situations like these. I didn't have time to feel nervous because I knew I had to step up in that role and just do it. That road trip was huge for me and my confidence. I handled the ball well and was able to get the job done and we won both games while in Texas.

A reporter in Columbia named Darren Hellwege who covered Mizzou women's basketball had interviewed me tons of times during my career. Once when we were reflecting over my career, he felt the game at Saint Louis University was my "breakout" game. SLU was our very next game when we returned from the Texas road trip. I think Darren saw it as my breakout game because I went 4-for-4 from the three-point line and finished with 16 points in just my third college game. The shots I hit were also made at key times in the game when SLU was going on a run. It was a small dose of what was to come over the course of my career, hitting big shots in key moments and scoring threes in bunches.

*** *** ***

I will never forget my first career start as a Mizzou Tiger. We traveled to Texas to take on the University of Texas. It seemed like almost every other week we were headed somewhere to Texas because of all the Texas schools in the Big 12. To me, it really didn't matter if I was starting or not, I just wanted to play and to do my very best when I was out on the floor.

I also wanted to do so well that Coach would have to leave me out there. We lost that night, but I remember on the plane ride home, I had a special moment with Coach Porter when I was walking down the aisle toward my seat. I felt a hand grab my left arm. Coach Porter pulled me down and whispered in my left ear, "You got your foot in the door, now bust it open."

I remember going to my seat and just playing those words through my head and nodding because he was right. It was my time to step up. That moment was something that stuck with me for the rest of my playing days and still does to this day. Coach Porter was always what my parents called "a Morgan Eye fan." He saw the potential in me even when I didn't believe it myself.

Becoming a starter did not solidify my spot on the

team or make me superior to others. It was not a moment of relief where I could relax and take a step back as if I had "made it." Becoming a starter, and Coach Porter's words, only motivated me to work even harder. I remember Coach P telling me one time later in my career. She said, "It's not about who starts the game. It's about who finishes it." She meant that when it came to crunch time, to winning time, she wanted her fiercest competitors out there. I wanted to make sure that I was finishing every single game.

*** *** ***

**M**y **freshman year** was tough, to say the least. Along with battling my own self-doubt early, we didn't necessarily have the best season as a team. Our nonconference record was good and we only lost one game, but

It took a while for me to gain some confidence as a freshman, but I guess that isn't all that uncommon for first-year players at that level.

our team struggled when we began Big 12 play. We only won two regular season conference games that year. But we did beat Oklahoma State in the first round of the Big 12 tournament, which was good. I remember multiple conversations with Coach P throughout the season and her asking me, "Are you good? I know losing can be tough, especially when you come from a high school that is used to winning. It's all a part of the process." Some days it was really hard, but that word "process" was what kept me going. Sometimes I hated hearing the word but I understood it came along with that other word that Coach Porter told me—patient!

After that season, I was thirsty for more and past the stage of self-doubt. Through the middle of the season, I really came into my own. Only a few days after our season had ended, Kyley and I were back in the gym getting some shots in. Coach P came into the arena and chatted with us. Coach P often came down and chatted and rebounded while we got some shots up. She said to me, "You know, not everyone does that." I asked, "Does what?" She replied, "Gets it. Sometimes freshmen take a little longer, but you were able to get there and turn the corner."

Looking back on it today, several years later, and now I know what Coach meant by that conversation. I see freshman all the time who get challenged by the coaches just like I did. Sometimes the girl "gets it," and is able to come into her own. Others take a little more time and blossom into their next year, or sometimes longer.

It is, as Coach P says, a process.

# 19
Chapter

**I** **once heard a** television commentator mention how exciting it was to see players grow from their freshman year to their sophomore year, the year in their career where they made the biggest jump. From a statistical standpoint, my sophomore season was the best of my career. Do I think it was my best year, or that I was the best I could be when I was a sophomore? No. I had a lot of awards and accolades that year, but I was nowhere the player or leader or person I became by the time I was a senior. My sophomore year, I made the big jump in performance and teams started to take notice.

During the summer, we got to go home for three weeks before the summer session and three weeks at the end. It wasn't considered vacation time, though, because it was a time to get better as a player. I heard Coach Norton once say something about how fun it was to see someone transform their game over a summer. I took that to heart. I wanted to go home over my breaks and I wanted my transformation to be clearly visible. I wanted my coaches to know that the drills we did in our individual sessions, I went home and worked to master them.

It was never in my nature to sit still, either. During my freshman season, we all read one motivational book that appealed to us and I chose Tim Tebow's book, *Through My Eyes*. I have a lot of respect for Tim Tebow, the Heisman Trophy-winning quarterback from the University of Florida, and gained even more respect after reading this book. He spoke of a mantra he had and it really stuck with me. I used it to help push myself. The mantra stated: "Somewhere he is out there, training while I am not. When we meet, he will win." Without even knowing it, I was living out this mantra. I thought back to being in grade school and high school and how I would always be outside practicing on my court because I hated the idea of anyone working harder than me. I couldn't bear the thought of someone practicing while I wasn't.

I worked out at my old high school in Montrose, and my cousin Kendall, who went on to play college basketball at Rockhurst University in Kansas City, worked out with me a lot. Most people would probably laugh at the "weightlifting facility" or even the size of my gym. But the weight room had dumbbells, a bench, barbells, and everything I needed to perform my workout. My gym had the same size baskets and basketballs, so it would do just fine. The only downfall was working out in that summer heat in a gym with no air conditioning. (They have AC at Montrose now, those spoiled kids.) Now I am the old gal who gets to say, "Well, when I used to play ..."

I lifted three times a week and also did my conditioning in the gym. Sometimes I did sprints, other times a jump-rope workout, and sometimes long-distance running outdoors. Then I did my basketball work on the court. I created a lot of basketball workouts, and Kendall did them with me on most days.

I really took advantage of the summertime to get better at ball-handling skills, jump shots and things of that nature. When the season rolled around, I was ready.

*** *** ***

At first, it was hard for me to completely accept my role as a three-point shooter. When I was asked if I have always been able to shoot the ball, I say, "I have always taken pride in that, but I don't consider myself just a three-point shooter. I am going to shoot it when I am open, whether it's three feet from the basket or thirty."

In high school, I was able to do a little bit of every-thing—handle the ball well, set up a teammate for a shot, take a defender one-one-one, get to the rim, anything. I know most people are probably thinking, "Well, you played against 1A competition." Yes, that's true, but also remember that I played in a lot of competitive leagues in the summer and was still able to do those things. At the end of the day, I did have to be honest with myself that I was limited in certain ways when it came to athleticism, speed, and strength. I also knew my team needed some-one who could shoot the ball and that just so happened to be one of my greatest strengths—so I took my greatest strength and I honed in on it. If I was going to be a three-point shooter, then you bet I was going to be the best one there was.

It's important to note, even though I was known for shooting the ball, I still worked on developing my entire game. During the season, I spent most of my time getting up shots on the gun and making my release quicker. In the summer, when I would go home I had no gun to shoot on, so I used that time to focus a lot more on drill work with handling the ball, making moves with the ball, my floater, and my jump shot. I didn't worry so much about the volume of shots I got because this was my opportuni-ty to work on other elements of my game. The offseason is when I could try out new things and develop different elements of my game.

*** *** ***

Joshua Medcalf had an influential impact on my ca-reer as a player and in my personal life as well. Joshua is the founder of Train to Be Clutch and author of the book,

*Burn Your Goals.* He has written more books since, but this was the book that our team read and discussed when I was a sophomore.

Basically, what his business does is offer tools for mental training. For his visit, he obviously geared his efforts toward the perspective of an athlete. Joshua came to talk to our team and did a presentation on how to develop our mental game. I had never heard of any training tools to develop my mental game as a high school player, so I really didn't know what to expect. I wasn't sure what to think. I had only been somewhat introduced to "thinking right in sport" because of Dr. Rick McGuire and his program, Positive Coaching, at the University of Missouri. Joshua came in confident and told us his story. It was very impactful, to say the least.

Some of the major points I remember surrounded the concept of "burning your goals." I found that interesting because as athletes we were always told to set goals for ourselves. We set goals in the weight room, in our diet plan, and in the classroom. He also made sure to distinguish the difference between a goal and a dream. I could have said it was my goal to play to Division I basketball, but it would probably be more appropriate to say it was my dream. A dream, as he defined it, is something that you have wanted deep in your heart for a long time. Goals are something we set, and when we don't achieve them, it can lead to a downward spiral really fast.

Instead, what Joshua encouraged us to do was to focus on one day at a time—to control the things that we could control. If you tried your absolute best to be in the present, and be the best you can be that day, then you will eventually see results. Winning a basketball game was an end result and ultimately a goal—which was out of our control. The thing that was within our control were things like our attitude, our effort, and our hustle. If we shifted all of our energy on the controllables instead of whether we had more points than the other team on the scoreboard, then we could be satisfied with whatever the result was.

Joshua also told us a story about his days as a collegiate soccer player. Joshua explained the time when he was first introduced to visualization. He said he was even skeptical at first, so he decided to test the theory. He had never scored a goal off a header, which is using your head to direct a shot. He decided he would visualize himself doing so, and spent roughly ten minutes every day visualizing himself scoring a goal by using his head. He did this for two weeks, and then soon after in a game, the opportunity arose and he headed the ball into the net for a goal. The very next weekend, he did it again. In that short time, he had trained his brain to be able to do it, so when it happened in a game, it was as if he had already done it before.

What I have learned from more research is there is a part of our brain that doesn't know the difference between practicing—or visualizing—a move and actually physically performing it. Therefore, you can actually practice a move all in your mind, and that part of your brain won't know the difference.

Joshua Medcalf's visit was definitely a big defining moment for me and my journey in laying a foundation for visualization and for developing mental toughness. Luckily, our team had resources just across the street at the MATC. Dr. Scotta Morton served as our team's sports psychiatrist for three years of my career. What was very cool to me was that everything Scotta was teaching us went hand-in-hand with what Joshua had spoken about. We learned about tons of different ways to help us think right in sport.

For example, "next play." The game of basketball is

a game of mistakes. Whenever I would make a mistake, I had to quickly remind myself "next play." It was important to learn to refocus your mind after making a bad play. Some players write something on their shoes, others may clap their hands or physically act as if they are wiping the play off with their hands. These are all good examples of what we called "refocus routines." For my reminder, I naturally clapped my hands, but I also would snap my head band. It was a quick flick and I had to let it go. You never want a good play or a bad play to keep you from making the next play. To go along with reminding yourself of "next play," it's always good to follow that with a positive affirmation such as, "I got this" or "the next shot is going in." It's amazing the difference in your performance when you feed your mind the positives instead of the negatives.

I had a coach once put negative self-talk and positive self-talk into a good example. If I had a teammate who I knew was a great shooter and she just missed a shot, as a teammate, what would I say to her? Most likely I am going to tell her, "Hey, you've got that. Keep shooting. We need you. The next one is going down." So if I miss a shot, why am I saying things to myself such as, "Gosh, I suck. I can't hit anything?" I'm certainly not going to yell those things at a teammate for missing because I truly believe in them, so why would I say those things to myself? The lesson here is to be a good coach to yourself as well. You have to feed yourself the positive stuff.

I also learned it's impossible not to let negative thoughts creep into your mind. As humans, we have thousands of thoughts throughout the day. What I learned though, your mind can only focus on one single thought at a time. If I have a negative thought, all I have to do is replace that negative thought with something positive. It seems really simple, and it is when you break it down this way. Your thoughts are controlled by you, and you decide which thoughts to entertain.

Visualization is something that I bought into whole-heartedly. I was empowered by Joshua Medcalf and his story and the team time we had with Scotta in developing our mental skills. Coach P was a big advocate for the power behind developing mental toughness, so if she wanted us to do our visualization, I was always going to do it. For me, it was always an accountability factor and I was going to do it for my team. I always did most of my visualization at night before I went to bed. I thought about things I needed to work on and visualized myself doing it.

At night, I would take myself through both offense and defense. Defensively I saw myself in a low stance, knees bent, arms pointing at my man and the ball, my head is on a swivel, I am talking to my teammates through rotations "I got your help," "Skip pass!" or "I got ball!" I mentally practiced my closeouts when the ball got swung to my man. I close out on my man with high hands, short choppy steps and I am ready to take a big step in whatever direction they go. When the shot goes up, I contest with my hand through their face and turn around and box out, ready to grab a rebound.

Offensively, I would take myself through our plays. I made sure to set up my defender, made sure they thought I was going one way and then explode in the opposite direction, rubbing off the shoulder of a teammate setting a screen. I come in low, planting my inside pivot foot, hands up, the pass is timed perfectly into my hands, and I let it fly right off my fingertips with perfect rotation in the air. I jump straight up and land straight down, holding my follow through. I continue watching the ball until it goes right into the basket, nothing but net. I visualized a ton of me just shooting and the ball going into the basket, swish, swish, swish, every single time. It's interesting, if I go and shoot some baskets, the ball often goes where I picture it going. So if I shoot the ball and I see it a little right, it goes right. If I see it a little left, it goes left. If I see it short or long, it will go short or long. I got to where each time I just had to train myself to "see it" going in every single time I shot it. The ball will go where you see it going.

This reminds me of another mental tip I picked up from Dena Evans, who runs the Point Guard College Camp (PGC). Dena Evans is a well decorated women's basketball player herself and I had the opportunity to learn from her by attending the PGC camp going into my sophomore season. I actually learned this specific tip from a YouTube video I saw on PGC's Twitter handle some time after attending the camp. Dena talked about the "yes shot." Essentially the "yes shot" is all about finding that perfect feel for your shot. So first you have your word for when you shoot the perfect shot. This word could be "yes" or "money" or "smooth," something like that. For me, I always just said "yes."

I know some people think that "positive self-talk" or "visualization" or "thinking right in sport" all may sound like fluff, but it absolutely works. As a girl who would be picked dead last for the team of SEC guards if based solely on athletic ability and skills, I'm here to testify that it made me better. What can't be seen by physical appearance alone is all of the mental preparation I put in on my own time. I am a firm believer in visualization and mental toughness. It is one of the core reasons I was able to be successful at such a high level.

*** *** ***

Another form of visualization that I utilized was

what was called a Think Right Video. Our team was introduced to this idea from our sports psychologist, Scotta. Think Right Videos were something that other sports teams at Mizzou were using to help them get their minds right for games. Scotta shared an example of a Mizzou baseball player's video. His video was geared toward what motivates him to go out and perform at his best. The videos can be more serious or funny, or a combination of both. After watching the video, I knew right away I wanted to have one for myself for game days. Like I said, I fully bought in to the idea of visualization and the benefits it could have on my game.

Our video coordinator, Mike Donovan, told our team that he would be willing to put together videos for anyone who was interested. We just simply needed to give him material we wanted and maybe an idea of the "feel" of the video we wanted it to have. He would add all video clips of us playing.

The first video I had was my junior year. I knew I wanted to have some quotes, Bible verses, pictures, and things to remind me to have fun. Mike Donovan put the video to a country song, which was definitely my personality. The song was "The Only Way I Know" by Jason Aldean. It was perfect for the background of the visuals of me swishing shot after shot. I do believe watching the video before every game gave me a good boost of confidence taking the floor.

For my senior video, I knew what to expect from a Think Right Video and knew exactly what I wanted to add to it. I chose a voice-over that I found to be very powerful and telling of my career. The voice-over is from a well-known coach and trainer named Alan Stein. The video first begins with the words, "Success is not an accident. Success is a choice." The video then begins with clips of me during summer workouts and all the behind-the-scenes work in the weight room and outside running up the hill. During these clips, the voice-over plays:

> *"If you want to make it in this game, you have to do three things. You need to work hard, you need to work smart, and you need to work consistent. But you have to have all three. See, if you work hard and you work smart, but you don't do it very often or you don't do it consistently, you won't make it. If you work really really hard and you do it all of the time but you don't work smart, you're not going to make it. And it goes without saying, if you don't work hard, you don't stand a chance."*

Those words spoke so much truth to me. I also felt that those three things were reasons why someone like me was able to be successful at the highest level of collegiate basketball. Work hard, work smart, and work consistent. In the voice-over, Coach Stein goes on to explain what working hard really means. He explains:

> *"It's a relative term. Each of us defines it differently. What you consider working hard might make him laugh. What he considers working hard, Kobe Bryant might laugh at. So here is how I am going to define working hard. You take yourself to the point of discomfort. That could be physical, that could be mental, that could be emotional. But you take yourself out of your comfort zone. If you guys want to make it, you have to learn to be comfortable being uncomfortable."*

I had never thought about how each individual person can have their own interpretation of working hard. I think Coach Stein puts it best by saying working hard can be defined by stretching yourself to the point of discomfort, whether it be physical, mental, or emotional. The last lines of the voice-over states, *"Dream big. Work hard. Stay humble."* It was a mantra I felt I had been living during my playing career—a dream to play Division I collegiate basketball, an unsettling desire to push myself past my limits, and to always remember who I am and where I came from, no matter the success I may encounter.

My video starts off a little heavy and very sobering, but then it's time to pick things up to get me a little more pumped for game time. The words on the screen read: "Are the habits I have today on par with the dreams I have for tomorrow?" Of course, I have to put something that I consider humorous in my video because I like to laugh, smile, and have a good time. Therefore, I have the sound clip from the basketball scene in the movie The Cable Guy starring Jim Carrey. For anyone who hasn't seen the movie, basically Jim Carrey shows up to play pick-up with the guys and he shows up dressed with '90s short shorts and fully equipped with sweat bands. He tells the guys, "Got to warm up, don't want to pull a hammy." He begins running sprints on the court, touching each line. As he hits each line he shortens his distance until he's touched each line and sprints to the end of the court. Then he says, "Let's get it on."

I promise it is a lot funnier than I described. Anyhow, this scene plays during a clip of me warming up with my team. Then the clip takes you to the weight room where I am getting ready to test my approach vertical, which wasn't my strong suit. My head is pounding to the beat of the music that you assume is being played in the weight room. My eyes catch that the camera is on me and I crack a cheesy grin and squint my eyes. I turn to a nearby teammate, probably to crack a joke about my insane vertical that he is about to catch on video (total sarcasm). I take a deep breath and you hear the words, "Let's get it on!" It made me smile each time this part of the video came on. I wasn't known for my vertical jump, but it never stopped me from doing my best. I also wasn't too proud to poke fun at myself because at the end of the day I could still play ball regardless of how high I could jump.

The video then begins with music and me coming off the bench for starting lineups. The song I chose was Centuries by Fall Out Boy. I fell in love with the song because I felt that it encompassed leaving a legacy and as a senior. that's exactly what I wanted to do. Some of the lyrics read:

> *Some legends are told*
> *Some turn to dust or to gold*
> *But you will remember me*
> *Remember me, for centuries*
> *Just one mistake*
> *Is all it will take*
> *We'll go down in history*
> *Remember me for centuries*

My game highlights are shown during the song. This is when I really start to raise what we learned to call our arousal level. As athletes, it is our responsibility to find our optimal arousal level in which we compete at our absolute best. We were taught to learn our arousal level by using a scale of one to ten, with one being very calm and ten jumping off the walls. Using contrasting examples to explain, consider a sport such as golf, where the player needs to be fairly calm and in control of his/her movements probably operates on the lower end of the spectrum. A football player, on the other hand, may jump around banging his helmet on a locker to get fired up to go hit somebody. I felt I always operated during games at around a six or seven. There were points in time where my arousal level may get higher, and other points where

I will bring myself down, such as when I was shooting a free throw. My video helped me get in my zone. It starts off very calm and then builds up into getting me hype.

Some of my favorite Bible verses and quotes are sprinkled in throughout. One of my favorite Bible verses is 1 John 4:18, *"There is no fear in love. But perfect love drives out fear…"* That verse was brought to my attention by my teammate, Lianna Doty. It really helped to put in perspective that there is no reason for me to ever fear failure on or off the court. I am perfectly loved by God no matter what, and His love casts out all fear.

Another verse I enjoy is from 2 Timothy 1:7, *"For the Spirit of God gave us does not make us timid but gives us power, love and self-discipline."* I really like this verse first because what it makes me think of is to never shy away from greatness. God gave us all gifts and he wants us to shine bright.

The final thirty seconds of my video again uses a voice-over. This time it is from the famous speech given by the great coach, Jim Valvano. I always found him to be very inspiring and his words couldn't ring more true that in life, every day we should always think, laugh, and cry. "That's a full day. That's a heck of a day," he said.

As the voice-over ends, the final quote I read before taking the court comes from one of my assistant coaches at Mizzou who coached me my freshman and sophomore seasons. Coach Randy Norton always used to tell me, "Do your best, let God do the rest."

# 20
## Chapter

**D**uring my second year as a Mizzou Tiger, I was much more comfortable in my role on the team. I put in a lot of work in the offseason, understood our program's expectations, and understood all the terminology, I was feeling like part of the team, and was finally playing more free. Because I got in the gym so much and was constantly getting in shots, I earned what people call the "green light" to shoot the ball. I still had to learn and understand the importance of time and score, and good shot versus great shot, but my coaches and teammates wanted me to shoot it.

I recall a time when Kyley Simmons set me up for pitch action in transition. I was sprinting down the right lane of the court, she was pushing the ball just behind me, and our eyes got big — we both knew what we wanted to do. She dribbled right at my defender, screened her off and tossed me the ball. I slightly fumbled the ball, so I chose not to let it fly. Kyley was mad as she shouted "Shoot it!" I can't blame her either, because she did a lot of work to set me up for a good shot. But now I laugh at those times because who wouldn't want their teammates getting mad if you DON'T shoot it. I had no reservations about shooting the ball, but if I didn't, it was simply because I lost the grip and wasn't "feeling it."

One particular night I was definitely "feeling it." We talk with our sports psychologist about flow, and I was certainly in a flow that game. Our opponent for the evening was Tennessee-Martin. They played a lot of zone

After hitting a three-pointer, I loved giving a little fist pump every now and then. It became something of a trademark.

against us, and as someone who likes to shoot, I loved when teams would zone us. I ended up knocking down eight three-pointers that evening. It was a record for most threes made in a game in Mizzou women's basketball history. I didn't do anything different in my preparation for that game, I didn't do anything out of my capabilities. I simply focused on one play at a time, my teammates constantly screened for me, and gave me great looks at the basket. I actually have a scar on my right bicep from that game—I think a girl scratched me with her nail when she contested a shot. It's a baby scar, but I think about that game every time I see the scar. I think about how that game was just the start to a really unforgettable career.

*** *** ***

**M**y sophomore year was the year Mizzou made the switch from the Big 12 to the Southeastern Conference. I was skeptical of the switch at the time, but after experiencing playing in the SEC, it doesn't get much better than that. In women's basketball, the SEC is arguably the toughest conference in the nation. The athleticism and talent is unmatched.

It was time for our SEC home opener. We had just experienced our very first SEC game at Georgia, and it was ugly. I think Coach P has been on the record saying, "They took us to the woodshed." That was actually probably putting it nicely, because we absolutely got slaughtered. Those girls were all so fast, strong, and athletic. We felt rushed in everything we tried to do on offense. It was a big "Welcome to the SEC" moment.

But now it was our turn to play at home and we were ready to learn from the previous game and move on. One thing Coach P would always say after adversity would strike was, "All I know how to do is roll up my sleeves and go to work." She never allowed us to feel sorry for ourselves, not for one second. Auburn was quite a bit different than Georgia. Georgia played a very aggressive, up-in-your-face man defense while Auburn played a zone, and they were long, lanky, and athletic in that zone.

I like to use another one of Coach's sayings when I hear a team is going to zone us, "I am licking my chops." I knew I was going to get open looks, I just had to be ready to knock them down. Well, I had plenty of opportunities to knock down shots and that's what I did. I went 11-for-18 from three-point land. It was the most points I ever scored in a game—33 points, and all from behind the arc. Just like that, a few weeks after setting the Mizzou women's basketball record for most threes made in a game (8), I set the bar higher with 11. (That record still stands.)

My sophomore season, I came out ready to play. I had the mindset that I was going to be the most consistent player that I could be. I would have one game where I would make five or six threes and I would think, "Okay, cool. Let's do it again." Even while in a game, I would get one to fall—it's always so sweet when the first one goes down—I just kept thinking to myself, "Do it again and again and again." That's why oftentimes at the end of a game, I could never tell you how many I had made because I was always thinking about making the *NEXT* one. I never let myself dwell too much on a good game because I wanted to prove myself that much more the next opportunity I got. In fact, the day after I set the record for most threes made in a game, I was in the gym the next morning shooting on the gun before heading to class. I remember just having the mindset that I was going to just keep getting better. Shooting slumps seem to be inevitable—believe me, I had my share—but when I got hot, I did my best to keep it that way. My sophomore year was a good example of that. I credit a lot of that to my mental preparation and visualization that I was learning and getting better at.

*** *** ***

**F**ollowing a bad loss at Texas A&M, our team was really in a bit of a slump. Coach P could feel our team had the potential to do some great things, but something was holding us back. After the loss, we hopped on the plane and arrived late in Columbia, probably close to midnight by the time we got to the arena. Coach Pingeton asked us all to meet in the practice gym. We all grabbed a chair and made a big circle around the tiger head in the center of the court.

Coach P opened the floor by talking about things that hold us back as players. She felt we had something inside all of us that we had never really opened up about and shared with one another. There were a lot of tears shed that night as many of us opened up to one another about our experiences.

It was the first time I opened up about how I still hold on to how I felt I disappointed my community by losing in the final four at state my senior year. With tears in my eyes, I told my Missouri teammates that "I let down my team, my town, my school, my community, but getting to play here gave me another opportunity."

It is something that fuels me every day. I had never really shared that with anyone and I don't think I personally knew how much it was still a part of me. I can't recall all that was said that evening, but I do know it was a special night and moment for our team that sparked a fire within us. Coach P laid out how much time we had left in the season as far as number of practices, off days, game days, etc., and when you took all of that into consideration, you are left with a very small number. She challenged us to get in the gym more—and we all did. We made it into a fun competition to see who was in the gym the most. From that night on, some special things started to happen.

Our next opponent was Florida, which was ranked in the top 25. We were hosting the game and we felt as close as we had been all season. We had all committed to extra time in the gym and it was about to pay dividends. We focused on the process that game, taking it one possession at a time, and we ended up winning.

It was a very big deal to get a win over a nationally ranked opponent. Wins against top-25 opponents were a big deal for our program in laying a foundation for where we wanted to get to. It would not happen overnight, but we had to focus on the process and the things that we could control.

Our next test was against the well-respected Tennessee Lady Vols, an established program that set the standard for women's basketball. They are such a storied program that it was always a game I looked forward to playing in. The great Pat Summitt was no longer their head coach, but was still Head Coach Emeritus. We played Tennessee early in the season in Knoxville and got knocked on our butts, 84-39. Regardless, it was an amazing experience to play in their arena. I remember we were toward the end of our practice, just getting in some extra shots, and all of a sudden there she was. Coach Summitt was walking across the baseline to the opposite tunnel. I stopped bouncing my basketball, stopped dead in my tracks, and I whispered to Kyley, knowing she was a die-hard Summitt fan, "Kyley ... Kyley ... Look!" I imagined we looked like deer in the headlights as we slowly turned our heads and followed her every move. Coach Summitt is a legend. What she did for women's basketball is amazing and even though I didn't meet her, just seeing her was

126

a special moment for me.

Feeling fueled after our big win against Florida, we were feeling very confident heading into our home game against Tennessee. There was something special in the air that day, from shoot-around, to pregame meal, to chapel, to warmups, and finally tip time. Coach Porter, as usual, performed our team chapel after we finished our pregame meal. The story he decided to share for the day was David and Goliath. It was very fitting as we went into the game as David, the underdog. Tennessee rolled in as the un-tamed giant, Goliath. It is still one of my most memorable chapels because of how everything was about to unfold.

As we ran through the tunnel for the final time before the tip, the arena was full. I had never played in front of

Beating a storied program like Tennessee was one of the highlights of my career at Missouri, because we could see that we were making progress as a program.

127

so many people. Our fans really came out to support us on that Sunday afternoon. We weren't perfect that day, but what I do remember is how when one of us made a mistake, a teammate rushed over to tell you, "Next play!"

I had a pretty good game that day. I went 8-for-14 from the floor, shooting 6-for-12 from the three-point line and 4-for-4 from the free throw line. Our motion offense was hard to guard with all of our screening action and my teammates continued to screen for me. I got some timely threes to fall. There was also a specific play where I was running off a down screen, received a pass with a defender right on my tail, and I gave a quick head fake and was off into the lane. I let my floater fly — and nothing but net. It's a funny moment now because I never really shot floaters in games. I knew I was capable of doing it, but we were really disciplined to never go off of one foot so as not to draw an offensive foul. After that game, the floater started to become one of my go-to shots when I got near the bucket. There is also a picture that captured the shot. I like to think of the image as my version of Michael Jordan's "the shot."

We started to pull away in the second half. Lianna Doty shared a memory she had from the game. She said we were probably up by about ten points and I was taking the ball out of bounds. As I passed the ball to her to bring it up the court I said, "Let's get one right here." She remembered that moment because we were up by ten and could have taken it easy. In the moment, I knew we needed to keep executing. We could not let up against a team like Tennessee. It's a forty-minute game. We were so focused on each and every possession. From her recollection, we indeed did score on that possession.

For the first time in my career, I actually realized that the announcer says, "one minute remaining." When he said that, I finally let myself smile. We were actually going to slay Goliath. We beat Tennessee big that day, 80-63. The celebration was one to remember as we all ran to meet one another at center court, hugging, smiling, and yelling—some of my favorite pictures are from the victory that day.

In the locker room, we continued yelling and hugging as more and more teammates entered the room. We finally took our seats, waiting patiently for our coaches to enter the room. Coach P entered around the corner and the celebration ensued once again. When we finally settled down, Coach P addressed our team. With tears in her eyes, she told us how proud she was of us. She said, "We talk a lot about laying a foundation for this program, and you just laid a whole layer down." It really was a big step for the direction we wanted our program to go, because back-to-back victories against two ranked opponents was huge.

That game is still something my old teammates, coaches, and I talk about today. It wasn't just because we beat Tennessee, but it was everything that went into that day. If you ask any of the players or coaches, they will tell you there was just something magical about the day. It was a big part of laying the foundation for the Mizzou women's basketball program and its future.

*** *** ***

We ended the 2012-13 season with an overall record of 17-15. We won five conference games in our first year in the SEC. Winning games is tough, period. But winning games in the SEC, well, it makes things just that much tougher. However, with our winning record, we were eligible for postseason play. We received a bid to the WNIT Tournament. It was the first postseason tournament for our program since 2005-06. It was the next stepping stone in "the process" that Coach P often referred to. It was refreshing to start seeing some of our hard work pay off. It wasn't the NCAA Tournament, but we had the opportunity for our program to take the next step and to play more basketball.

We hosted the first round of the WNIT against Eastern Illinois. I can't really recall many details from that game other than the fact that we lost. It was a devastating loss, to say the least, especially since we were at home. Eastern Illinois was a veteran team and we were young and inexperienced as it pertained to postseason play. Any loss is hard, but the last one of a season is always particularly hard because you know it is your seniors' last game of their careers. It was the last game I played with my first roommate in college, Liz Smith. It was the last game I played with my roommate during my freshman year, Liene Priede. It was the last time I would play with Sydney Crafton, a four-year player at Mizzou and had seen Mizzou at some of its hardest times. I loved those girls dearly and had so much fun getting to know them. It was a privilege to play with them and be around them every single day. They are forever my sisters.

*** *** ***

Little did I know it was also the last game that I would play with Kyley Simmons. Following the loss against Eastern Illinois, we headed for the locker room. Kyley was more than visibly upset—she was crying uncontrollably. I went over to console her, telling her, " This is only going to make us better. We still have two more years." She wouldn't stop crying. I thought maybe she was just really upset about our seniors leaving. It wasn't until the very next day that we found out about her intentions.

130

We had one final team meeting to wrap up the season and talk about postseason workouts to prepare for the next season. The meeting was set for 2 p.m. that afternoon. At about 1:50, most of our team was sitting on the couches in our locker room. When I noticed Kyley wasn't there, I texted her to remind her of our meeting. She didn't respond, which I thought was odd. At 1:55, I called. No answer. Everyone knows if you aren't at least ten minutes early for a meeting, you are late. When 2 p.m. finally came, there was no Kyley—and no coaches. That was very odd. After about ten minutes, we all started looking around at each other wondering what was going on. It was very unusual that the coaches weren't on time for a meeting. Finally, at about 2:30 p.m., we sent someone up to the office to see what was going on.

While we all sat on the couch, Bree Fowler made eye contact with me and said, "She wouldn't." I replied, "No way. Not without talking to us first." Bree and Kyley had had brief conversations about her wanting to transfer, but never thought it was anything to be worried about. Plus, we were all such great friends we never thought she would just spring this on us. The report from the office was that Kyley was meeting with our coaches and we needed to continue to wait downstairs. Well crap, this wasn't looking good. After what felt like an eternity, we heard the code on the locker room door being punched, the door swung open and Kyley entered with her usual smile and took a seat on the couch. The coaches followed behind, Coach P sat near the front and the assistants all filled behind the U-shaped couch we were sitting on.

Coach P wasted no time, she said, "Kyley, you want to go ahead." She gave the floor to Kyley and she got about a sentence out before I started crying uncontrollably. She had decided she wanted to transfer. One by one, the girls went and gave her a hug before she left the meeting. I remained sitting on the couch crying. I had so many emotions rushing through me at that moment that I couldn't even look at her. As one of her best friends, I was obviously devastated. This wasn't how things were supposed to happen. We came in together and we were supposed to leave together, too. We were going to help turn around this program and lay this strong foundation for its future success. I was so sad she was leaving, but I was also mad. I felt that the decision she was making was selfish. I just felt really hurt because I didn't want to lose one of my best friends. We did everything together. She was a major reason that I came out of my shell in college and went out and did things and met new people.

As you can imagine, the following weeks were very hard and awkward considering Kyley, Bree and I lived together in a house. Bree and I would be heading to workouts or getting home from workouts and Kyley was doing her own thing. It was almost even awkward if we saw one another on campus. I really hated how things were developing, and on move-out day, it still wasn't completely smoothed over. Kyley and I had had a couple of heart-to-heart talks that eventually led to crying. We thought we had resolved some of the issues, but there were still some tension. When move-out day came, I decided the best way I could leave things was to write Kyley a letter. I laid it all out there. I told her why I felt hurt and I was sorry for anything that I had done to hurt the situation. I wanted to leave that house with peace in my heart and hope that wherever she went she would be happy.

The reason I mention this story about Kyley is because I view it as a life-changing event for me. The day that Kyley told the team that she was leaving, we actually had the whole team over that night. It was somewhat of an awkward evening, but I had a little bit of one-on-one time with Liz Smith, who had just played her last game at Mizzou. I admired Liz so much because I felt she was so full of wisdom. That night she already seemed to find clarity in the whole situation of Kyley transferring and explained to me, "Mo, with Kyley leaving, you have a chance to step up as a leader."

That thought hadn't even crossed my mind. I was still in the crying, then mad, then "okay I'm fine" stages, and that cycle just repeated. Kyley was no doubt a vocal leader on our team but with her leaving, it certainly opened up an opportunity for me to be a leader—something I never would have dreamed I would be for a Division I program. With Kyley leaving, I also had to learn to branch out on my own and with my other friends. No doubt I made a lot of friends with Kyley here and I came out of my shell, but now it was up to me to be outgoing. I think in the grand scheme of things, I learned a lot about myself.

Kyley's decision to transfer was also very big for the program as a whole. There was a lot of room for growth in our program in the area of trust. The coaches were obviously unprepared for Kyley's decision, as were most of her teammates. On the positive side, it was an opportunity for us to look how we could build trust and make sure another situation like that wouldn't happen again.

Kyley and I have since reconnected from our Mizzou days. I think we are both thankful for the way things happened because it ended up being such a good learning experience. I can proudly say I look back at our time at Mizzou together and I remember all of the good times. We have since made a lot of good memories since graduating and continue to stay in touch.

I will always be grateful to her because she pushed me so hard our freshman year. I never thought my body was capable of running around so much. She helped me realize that I could raise the bar for myself much higher than I ever thought possible. She will forever be one of the most fun, crazy, most outgoing people I ever met at Mizzou and I always look forward to when we get to reconnect.

# 21
## Chapter

I think a lot of players can get caught up in minutes played or whether they get a starting position. For me, I just wanted to make the most of every opportunity I got on the floor. I wanted to play so hard that Coach P had no choice but to give me a chance. When I would get an opportunity, I wanted to play so hard that Coach also had no choice but to leave me in because I was impacting the game in some fashion—and that didn't always mean I was scoring.

I made five or more three-pointers in a game several times as a sophomore. I had the mindset that I just wanted to be as consistent as possible. If I got one shot to fall, it was on to the next shot. For the majority of that year I came off the bench as the sixth man in our rotation. Coach P made sure to have a conversation with me coming in as the sixth man to make sure I understood reasons why they were doing that. She assured me, "Don't think your entire career is going to be like that." I wasn't destined to always be a sixth man, not that there is anything wrong with that.

I was used as a spark off the bench when we needed scoring. It was working really well for us, so our coaches felt there wasn't any reason to change it. I personally was fine with it. Like I said, I just wanted to play and I didn't care when I got in the game but was always ready when my number was called. By the end of the season I was recognized with SEC honors as the Co-Sixth Woman of the Year. For me, that is a pretty big deal because the SEC is

arguably the best league for women's college basketball.
Every game you are going up against future WNBA and
professional basketball players. Any sort of recognition is
quite an honor and I was humbled to receive the award
that season.

*** *** ***

That season, I started to get some national attention
for consistently knocking down threes in our games. By
the end of the season, I was the NCAA statistical champion for most three-pointers made per game with 3.5.
Like I said earlier, I never considered myself a three-point
shooter, but if I was going to be classified as something
I was going to be the best at it—and that year I was the
best.

But let me be the first to say how it was only made
possible because of my coaches and my teammates.
That award is no individual award at all. My coaches
consistently put me in situations to get shots, and my
teammates tirelessly screened and rescreened for me to
get open. Basketball is a team sport and all awards are
made possible by the team. Still, it was a very, very cool
award to have as a girl who just dreamed to play Division
I basketball. To be No. 1 in the country in anything was
something truly special.

*** *** ***

I was getting ready to head to the arena for spring
workouts when I got a text from Coach P. She asked if
I could meet with her before individuals. Immediately, I start replaying the last couple of days, weeks, and
months, and I was wondering, what did I do wrong?
She wanted to meet five minutes before my individual

started. I am thinking maybe she forgot and I responded, "Yeah, I can meet. My individual starts at 2."

The only response I got back was, "I know what time individuals are." The response made me think "crap!" It seemed she was being short with me, but I was not sure why. I sat in the gathering area in Cornell Hall waiting for my class, breaking into a sweat because I had no idea what I did to make Coach mad. She was never usually short like that with her responses and it was not at all my intention to imply that she did not know when individuals were.

I made my way up the stairs to Coach P's office, scared of what my destiny held. I met Coach P's eyes and she gave no type of "warm" invite. Her face stayed like stone. She told me to have a seat. Then she went and grabbed the other coaches and asked them to come in. At this point, I was freaking out. I had no idea what this was about, I had no idea what I did wrong, I had no idea why Coach seemed so standoffish. As all of the assistant coaches filed into Coach P's office and took a seat, she proceeded with what the meeting was all about. She held an envelope in her hand. She began reading the letter, "Morgan Eye, congratulations, you have been invited to the USA World University Trials." I think they all expected a different reaction, but all I got out was, "Yeah, um … I got that letter too. It was on my chair yesterday, but I didn't know what it was."

Coach Norton responded with a giggle, "Mo, do you know what this is?" My coaches continued to tell me about the amazing opportunity. They explained how only 35 players in the entire country get invited. One criteria was you must have two years of eligibility left in college. Once they broke everything down to me, I was stunned. I may not have expressed as much excitement as I truly felt but everything hit me so unexpectedly. I couldn't believe the committee wanted me to try out. Now that I can sit back and reflect on that opportunity, oh my goodness, what an amazing blessing. Who would have thought, this little small-town farm girl was going to get invited to a USA trial to play basketball!? I can't even say it was something to cross off my bucket list, because it wasn't ever something I even dreamed about.

The day before heading out to the Olympic Training Complex in Colorado, I stopped by the office to tell my coaches goodbye. They had a big care package for me to take on my trip. It was filled with tons of my favorite snacks and my favorite part — the letters. Each of my teammates and coaches wrote me personalized letters wishing me luck at the tryouts. I remember each letter showed the personality of each individual. Some letters made me laugh, others made me cry. It was a particular moment, as I read each letter with tears in my eyes, that I knew God had truly blessed me with amazing people in my life.

Many letters wished me luck and told me I could do it! I recall Coach Rae Brown's letter. She wrote in her letter not to for one second allow myself to question whether or not I deserved to be there — it would be a waste of my energy to go down that road thinking that. Her message really struck me because, of course I had my doubts. I was going against the best of the best. She was right though, I had to control what I could control and that included my mindset going into the trials. I remember in Coach P's letter, she outlined the entire letter with inspiring words. Just seeing all of the time and effort she put into her letter meant the world to me. Something that I have learned about Coach P is to really respect what she says because she will never lie to you. So when she tells you just how proud she is of you, it hits a little different because you know she truly means it. Even writing about it years later,

I get teared up about this because sometimes I just can't believe how lucky I was to be able to come to Mizzou and be coached by this amazing woman.

After getting emotionally charged for my trip, I faced my next anxiety — traveling on a plane by myself. Okay, let's be honest, I come from a town that has no street lights and the most traveling I have done is always done with the team so I just follow the group in Mizzou gear not really paying attention to anything. Luckily, I got to fly out of the Columbia airport, which is equivalent to the size of a couple of restaurants smashed together.

As I went to board the plane, there were out-of-towners giggling at the size of the airport, and I actually found it more relaxing and less stressful. I literally sat in the very first seat on the small plane, which was taking us to Chicago's O'Hare International Airport. Luckily, I asked the flight attendant where I needed to go to connect on my flight to Colorado, and he was very helpful. I am not usually one to ask people questions when I am traveling, but I had to get over that because I didn't want to miss my connecting flight. Lesson here, it is okay to ask questions.

Upon arriving in Colorado, I checked in and was given my USA apparel. I got a USA backpack equipped with my practice jersey, a T-shirt, and hat. This was a really cool moment for me. I get to keep this, right? Even if I don't make the team? My roommates for the next couple of days were Aaryn Ellenberg from Oklahoma, who I remembered playing against my freshman season when we were still in the Big 12. My other roommate was Reshanda Gray from California. They were both really sweet girls, and it was fun to hang out with them.

I made my way down the halls, stopping every once in a while to introduce myself. I felt very out of place. So many of these girls already knew each other so well but this was my first time ever being invited to a USA trial.

I am sure the girls probably knew each other somewhat from their AAU days as well, which I had no experience. I made my way to one door that had a couple Tennessee players I recognized. I introduced myself, "Hey, I'm Morgan." I got a response from one of the Tennessee girls, "We know who you are." I think they were still salty from us beating them at home. I wasn't sure how to respond, but I think it was said in good fun, so I smiled and laughed it off.

The practices began, and I hated these types of environments, to be honest, feeling like you had to prove yourself in an unknown setting with girls you barely knew. It's hard to show what you are capable of when your own teammates don't even know you. It makes you feel like you not only have to prove yourself to the coaches, but also to your teammates. We did a variety of drills at the tryouts and, of course, scrimmages that took up most of the time.

Something that was hard for me to get used to was the painted lanes and blocks on the court. We were playing on a international court, so the lane was bigger and the three-point line was deeper. People who have seen me play know I have no problem shooting it deep, but what I have found about myself was that I really rely on the lines on the court to know how far I am from the basket. I may be making a cut and getting a feel for exactly where I am based solely on where the lane is or where the three-point line is, but here the calculation was thrown off. That's probably why I had a quick release because I already knew where I was on the court but here it was going to be a little different. It was something I had to make an adjustment to — all the girls had to.

To say the least, the one-on-one drills were not my strong suit. It never really has been. I did fine in all of the full-court drills. While a lot of the girls were huffing and puffing, I was ready to step up and go again. That credit goes to Coach Linn, who helped me get conditioned for the altitude in Colorado. We utilized the Hypoxico machine, which could simulate what it would be like to breathe in the thin Colorado air. Basically, I would put on this mask that made me look like Baine from the Batman movie and a tube connected to these air bubbles and then to a machine which would alter the air that I could take in. The work paid off though, as I found myself ready to keep running during the drills and scrimmages while others needed a break.

I didn't play terrible during the scrimmages, but I also don't feel like I did enough to stand out. I was a three-point shooter and that's why I got picked to attend this thing. I was the NCAA statistical leader in threes made per game that year. I didn't make enough threes to really turn heads in Colorado. Deep down, it bothered me because I am a competitor and I know what I am capable of. I just never was great at showcasing my skills at camps or tryouts. I thrived when I got to play with my team— whether that be growing up or in college. But tryouts are all part of the system and I fell short and didn't make the team. Let's not short-change that I was up against the best talent in the nation as well. I was fine with it. I knew I did my best, and what a great experience it was. Very well-deserved players made the team that year, including both of my roommates, Ellenberg and Gray.

I had the opportunity to play with some amazing players who went on to play professionally in the WNBA and overseas. Players like Cierra Burdick, Odyssey Simms and Shoni Shimmel, who treated me so nicely. She was at the camp with two of her teammates and they all invited me to sit and eat with them because they knew I didn't really know anyone. They were first class and I am grateful to have met them.

Even though I didn't get to represent the USA on the final roster, I still represented Mizzou and my hometown of Montrose to the best of my ability. It was an experience I will never forget and I have some pretty sweet USA gear I can show off to my kids and grandkids someday. I can tell them with pride how this small-town girl worked so hard and she got to try out for the USA World University Team.

# 22
Chapter

**W**hen **I reflect on** my junior season in 2013-14, I honestly don't remember a ton of moments that stood out to me. I was coming off of a record-setting sophomore season, but I was still hungry for more. I continued to work hard in the offseason and when I went home for breaks.

I never really let myself think too much about my accomplishments. I knew when it was all said and done, that I would look back and enjoy them. I wanted to be the best. I always remembered what Gil Hanlin had said to me and my team when we were little girls, "Once you think you're the best you can be, that is when you start declining." I did not have time to take a step back. I was only going to move forward. It was always a dream of mine to go "dancing" in the NCAA Tournament. I still wanted to keep working for that opportunity to compete in the biggest tournament in women's college basketball.

One of my best memories of that season was our Senior Night. Those are always tough in one way or the other. There are so many mixed emotions about that entire day because you can't get caught up in all of the "lasts" you are experiencing that particular day.

Senior night was for Bri Kulas and Tania Jackson, who was better known as T.J. She was unable to play that year because she had a long history of knee troubles, but she was every bit a part of our team. She had a voice like no other, and her energy for our team was so contagious. Even though she was unable to physically affect the game, she played a major role every single game by bringing her voice and her energy. Knowing she couldn't be out there was a big motivation to me as a player and her teammate to get a win for her.

Bri Kulas was our other senior. She had come from Johnson County Community College and this was my second season with her. She was a baller, no doubt. Bri would go on to be drafted in the WNBA at the end of the season—our first draft pick since my former teammate Christine Flores was drafted in 2012. Our opponent for the evening was Ole Miss. I recall it being a battle back and forth the entire game. Every game in the SEC was like that—you had to bring your absolute best no matter who your opponent. Coach P would always say about the com-

Pregame introductions were always very cool at Missouri, and I loved playing in front of all of our great home fans in Columbia.

petition in the SEC that on "any given night" something could happen. Records went out the window and you had to bring it.

The game was dwindling down to the last couple of minutes. Bri Kulas was called for a foul, her fifth and final foul. As soon as it happened, I looked up at the video board to learn it was her fifth foul. Lindsey Cunningham must have done the same thing because we both instantly had the same reaction of reaching out to our teammates and pulling each other in close and saying, "Hey, we are going to do this for Bri."

There was no way we were going to let Ole Miss spoil Bri and T.J.'s senior night. We were able to get the job done by making our free throws and a few defensive stops. That game was a cool moment for me because I think it really showed the culture that Coach P and her staff had built. We were all playing for a bigger purpose than ourselves—no selfish agendas, just laying it all out there for our seniors. That evening, both Bri Kulas and I also scored our 1,000th career points. Bri and I were interviewed after the game, and it felt good to stand next to one of our seniors and proudly say we got it done for them.

*** *** ***

One of the cool moments during the season was getting to play against my old high school rival Jordan Garrison. I always looked up to her for motivation as a small-town girl being looked at by Division I schools. I was always motivated to keep working hard because I too wanted to pursue a basketball career at a big-time university.

Jordan was playing at Creighton University in Omaha, Nebraska and, ironically, we played them in the first round of the WNIT Tournament that year. That game was played at Creighton, and I honestly hate that game, and I hate bringing up the memory of it because I played awful for my team. It was Bri's last game, and so it's hard to know that my focus and my performance was not up to par by any standards and we lost the game.

You never want any senior to go out on a bad game and that was what made that loss so painful. I can, however, look back now and appreciate the amazing opportunity it was to suit up one more time against a small-town "foe" like Jordan. I use the term "foe" loosely because we were never huge rivals or anything in high school, but playing against Jordan and the Osceola Indians was always a game our team looked forward to, as well as both communities because they were always competitive games.

I think for that particular game, our communities back home had something they could be very proud of. Jordan and I were both just small-town girls living our dreams on the biggest stage of women's basketball.

*** *** ***

My junior year was just okay for me, but I did some good things. I think I am always my toughest critic, so maybe I was better than okay. I made 106 three-pointers that year, which ranked me sixth in the nation in total threes made while finishing second nationally with 2.48 threes made per game.

Individual accomplishments aside, again our team did not make the NCAA Tournament. However, I remember that word Coach P always preached—the "process." Our program continued to build on our success from the previous seasons and we qualified for the postseason for the second season in a row.

# 23

Chapter

**I**n early October of my senior season (2014-15), we were finishing up with some of our last individual workouts before we would begin our official practices. Following the conclusion of a team individual, well-respected television analyst Deb Antonelli spoke with our team. She does a lot of color commentating on women's basketball games for ESPN, CBS and FOX, among others. Just watching her from afar, you can tell she is a very intelligent, strong woman and a great advocate for the women's game.

Each year we have a speaker come to teach our team ways to handle ourselves with social media, interviews, etc. Deb took everything a step up and really made the meeting about our team and explained how close we truly were to becoming a really great team last season. She had definitely done her homework prior to working with us. She wrote statistics on the board that compared us to the top teams in our league from the previous season. She put South Carolina and Tennessee's numbers up on the board and showed just how close we were to them. She further explained if each person could do a little more here and there, that those little things could be the difference in our team making the next big leap into the top half of our conference and get an invite to the NCAA Tournament.

If each person could commit to grabbing just one more rebound, or eliminating one of their turnovers, it could be the difference in putting us in the top of our league. Deb, herself, is on the committee who helps decide which teams get in and which teams are left out of the tournament, so her insight was very helpful.

The next number Deb wrote on the board was "108." She proceeded to ask me, "Morgan, do you know what that number means for you?" At first I said no. She shuffled through some of her papers as the wheels in my head started to turn. Then I thought, wait a second, and asked, "Is that the number of threes I need?" She responded by asking, "Threes for what?" I answered more specifically this time, "Threes to break the NCAA record?" Deb replied, "Go ahead and repeat that for everyone."

I did as I was told and immediately felt a rush of heat come over my body. I never liked talking about that kind of stuff. I only remembered that 108 was the magic number for me because I admittedly had researched it one time, but had only talked about it in front of my family. It was quite another feeling to be talking about the number with the team.

Deb further asked my teammates in the room, "Who would like to say that they played with the best shooter in NCAA history?" Hands immediately shot up all across the room. That moment made me feel so good, so loved, and so valued.

I wrote in my journal about the meeting: *"Kayla later asked if I felt pressure to achieve 108. I said no. I have never set out to break any of the records I have. I just go out and give my best and if it happens, it happens! My teammates and coaches are really the ones that make it all possible. I just want our team to be successful!"*

I sincerely meant everything I wrote concerning that record. I had multiple conversations with Coach P about the record and she always encouraged me just to go do my best because the records that I already held didn't happen because they were goals or dreams of mine, but rather because I just focused on the moment and did my very best. Does that mean the thought of breaking that record didn't hold heavy on my heart and mind at times? No. I definitely wanted the record. I wanted to be the best there ever was. I was going to play as hard as I could as a senior, and let the chips fall where they may.

# 24
### Chapter

**I was bound and** determined to make my senior season the best of my career. It was time for our program to make the jump from the WNIT to the NCAA Tournament. We had the pieces to do it, too.

However, God had a very different vision for our season than I did. It was not at all how I drew it up.

I am able to share a lot from my senior season because I kept a journal all year. In a lot of what follows, my journal entries are in italics. You wouldn't want to actually see my pages, because you couldn't read my chicken scratch.

It was quite an adventure, my senior year. Throughout my entire playing career, I have never had to deal with any sort of major injury. The worst I dealt with was a couple really bad sprained ankles. In October, we were about to have our final individual group workouts before regular practices would start the upcoming Monday. Our workout would look a little different on this day because we were actually going to be a part of a coach's clinic at our neighboring school, Columbia College.

We did our typical drills so everything would run smooth. Coach P was mic'd up that day so she could walk through and explain our drills to the crowd. We were in front of a packed gym and everything was going relatively smooth. We began our final drill of the practice plan, which consisted of a little bit of three-on-three. After we finished with that session, there was a little time remaining so Coach P let us continue playing.

I remember the play like it was yesterday. I was on offense, the ball got shot, it bounced long off the back of the

rim and toward the sideline beyond the three-point line.
I saw my teammate, Sierra Michaelis, coming for the ball
with Lianna Doty as a defender coming in hot pursuit.
In my mind, I was quickly calculating if Sierra would get
there before I did. That small hesitation led to the mishap.
Looking back, I feel I could have easily gotten to it with
no problem had I not hesitated, but I did. As I reached out
for the ball, both Lianna and Sierra met me in the chase of
the ball. A small nudge from Michaelis to Doty sent Doty
into my left knee, causing it to buckle slightly.

I heard a pop. The gym fell completely silent. I immediately closed my eyes and laid there as I thought the
worst. As the coaches and our trainer rushed over, I sat up
and smacked my hands to the court, knowing something
was wrong. As soon as my frustration showed, Coach Rae
Brown was right in my ear telling me not to let myself
go down that road of thinking negative things. She whispered, "Only positive thoughts, only positive thoughts."
I needed that in that very moment because I was about to
lose it fast. In that moment as our trainer, Alison, moved
my leg around and asked questions, I was taken back in
a time warp of the first time I experienced a bad ankle
sprain in the seventh or eighth grade. I remember wailing
on the floor, literally thinking my career was over.

Luckily, I was wrong and was able to walk off on
my own power. I remember the moment when I got up I
was thinking, "Oh, maybe this isn't that bad." It just hurt
so bad lying there. And so I thought maybe this was the
same situation. Maybe it won't hurt so bad and I can walk
off. Alison and Coach P helped me to my feet. We began
our walk from half court toward the training room as all
eyes remained on me. Right foot, left foot. Right foot, left
foot. Okay, it's not bothering me. Then all of a sudden, I
felt my knee buckle and I flinched. I just shook my head,
"No, something isn't right." Alison and Coach P put my

arms around their shoulders and carried me off the court.

I lay on the training table with tears in my eyes, terrified of what the diagnosis might be. Coach P was right by my side with tears in her eyes. She knew how hard I had worked, not just in the offseason, but in my entire career. It just didn't seem fair that something like this could be happening. Alison told me that Dr. Sherman, our team's physician, would meet us over at our arena. Alison put ice on it and I was able to walk to the car. I passed Doty on the way and I could see the concern in her eyes. I didn't know what the for sure diagnosis was going to be, but I was feeling better knowing I was walking on my own power, so I assured her I didn't think it was anything major.

Dr. Sherman tested my left knee to make sure that I didn't tear anything. All was good there—no tears. He ended up diagnosing me with a Grade 2 MCL sprain, and said I would be out four-to-six weeks. What did that mean to me? Well, I heard the "four weeks" and not the "six weeks." I started crying again. I knew practice was starting on Monday and I wanted to—no, I needed to— be there for my team.

Coach P settled me down, explaining that maybe this was all happening for a reason. "When was the last time you took actual rest?" I couldn't give a good answer. Maybe I would rest two or three days max when the season finally ended. I never wanted to get out of shape and I just could never sit still. She explained that maybe this was a good thing for my body, being a senior and all. I should've been thankful it was just a sprain and with the right rest and rehab, I would be back to full go by the start of our first game. Coach P further challenged me to remain mentally tough. She challenged me to practice my visualization, to see myself taking game shots at game speed. Since I wouldn't be able to shoot physically, she

153

told me to do my shooting visualization for as long as I normally came in to shoot, which averaged probably 30 minutes.

I did get somewhat lucky with the timing of all of this. I had already planned to go home for that weekend since the season would officially be starting on Monday with our first practice. My sister had just had her first baby, it was the perfect opportunity for me to sit around, ice my knee, and hold Ren all day long. I kept my injury on the down low, which believe me is not easy to do in a small town. I didn't want people concerned in any way because I knew I would recover fine and be back on the court in the "four weeks" that I heard the doctor say.

## RECOVERY TRAIL
### Journal entry 10/6

*My last first day of practice is in the books. It was in no way how I imagined it would be because I was on the sidelines. I would not let that stop me from making the most out of it! I encouraged and gave advice to my teammates the whole time and will continue to do that. I tried to visualize myself doing the same drills as I watched each player go through their rep. My teammates, overall, had a great first day!....*

*I have to say I have the best sisters in the world. I came to my locker today to find 3 notes hanging there! One from Doty, Jua, and a thank you note from Kay cuz I had left a post-it note on her car earlier that day to get her pumped for practice!*

I've said this before, but my love for my teammates is real. When we see someone knocked down, we pick each other up. We truly are a sisterhood. Writing

Post-It notes to one another was very common with this group of girls and I especially needed some encouragement because I was not at all used to being sidelined with an injury.

\*\*\*    \*\*\*    \*\*\*

I had never had any sort of serious injury in my life. This was by far the most serious for me, and it was only a sprain. I would be on crutches for a few weeks. I remember turning corners was really hard because I didn't have the strength to twist. Sudden movements in the shower would make me flinch because I twisted my knee a little too much. Getting into bed was very difficult because I didn't have the strength to lift my leg up to the bed. Alison taught me a trick days later. She explained to sit on the bed and use my good leg by scooping my right foot under my left ankle and cradle it up to the bed. It was so helpful.

Time seemed to be flying by and I felt I should be further along with rehab. I felt I should be lacing up and ready to play. I was nowhere near close to that. I had to do a lot of things on the sideline, including extra rehab sessions at the MATC and coming early to the arena whenever possible. Watching from the sideline is really hard to do because I so badly wanted to be out on the court with my teammates. They were going through all of the "hard stuff" that the early practices in the season usually require before practices lighten up when games begin. I hated watching them do all of those drills that I personally disliked. It sounds funny, but I felt like I was getting a free pass from having to go through those tough drills with them. There I was, on the sideline riding the bike or the versa climber.

There were a lot of days as I was riding the bike that

I started to feel myself losing my position as a leader on the team. It's hard to be a leader when you can't be physically on the court talking the game with your teammates because you have to focus on your rehab on the sideline. One day at practice, I was riding the stationary bike near the tunnel entrance, watching the girls compete in a full-court five-on-five drill. Nate Buxman, the director of Athletes in Action was in attendance that day, as he often would come and watch our practices. He walked over to me and asked, "Mo, how are you doing?" I gave the typical response that I was doing okay. Then he spit out some wisdom that I had not really thought about. First, he reinforced to me that God has a plan. Then he challenged me to really find my value.

I needed to understand that I'm not just "Mo the basketball player" because right now, I can't play, so what does that make me? He further encouraged me to watch my teammates and see different reactions and how I could encourage and pick them up. Finally, he said, "This is a great way for you to see qualities in teammates who could step up and be leaders too, something that will become very valuable come February." Wow, I hadn't thought about any of that at all. Here I was just feeling sorry for myself because I felt distant from the team. As I contemplated what Nate said, I really could see some of my teammates step up in different ways, filling the void that I had left. As much as I loved being a leader for the team, I couldn't do it alone. And as athlete knows, the day comes when the ball quits bouncing.

Visualization would be a key for me to stay game-ready. I did a lot of my visualization while I was icing my knee. I would take myself through different shooting routines and just see the ball go swish, swish, swish. Mike Donovan also put all of my makes from my junior year onto my tablet so I also utilized visualization by watching all of my made shots. When I was on the sidelines, I put myself in my teammates shoes as if I was performing the same drill as them. It was a way for me to stay focused and involved with practice.

As I continued my recovery, I kept insisting to Alison that I was ready to try more. I wanted to start trying to perform lateral movements. Little by little Alison gave in and let me at least try it. I was chomping at the bit because I wanted to play and I felt I was supposed to be back out there playing by now. But patience is a virtue, right? I really was starting to feel a ton better. I know early on I had days I just wanted to cry because I never thought I was going to be the same again. But eventually, I would get back to full strength and back on the court with my team.

My recovery kept coming along, slowly but surely. I kept getting to add more and more as the days progressed. Luckily, Mizzou has many resources available for rehab. I was able to start running on a machine called Alter G. Basically, you put on this thing that feels like a ballet tutu and it is connected to a treadmill and air is filled into it so that your complete body weight is not on your joints. It is literally like running on air. Each time as I got stronger, we could increase my speed and the body weight I would put on my joints.

Finally, I was able to do some individual shooting workouts with Coach Porter and that felt really good just to get game-like shots in. By the third week after my accident, I returned to drills with the team, but could not perform any contact drills. The biggest thing for me would be just to shake off the cobwebs and get the timing of everything down again. For the most part, I did a good job of keeping my conditioning. However, any basketball player will tell you, there is a difference between being in shape and being in basketball shape. When I was able to run more and do drills, I remember my calves just being on fire and so sore.

Of course, to me, it was a good sore.

*** *** ***

As it goes, this particular season would not only require people to step up in leadership roles, but in roles that they may otherwise not have played in. Another unforeseen incident happened during the early weeks of practice. From my vantage point, we were in the practice gym and I again was on the stationary bike on the sideline. Our team was working on our offense against our scout team in the half-court. Lianna Doty was dribbling close to the baseline, planted her foot, and went down. It was a typical basketball play that she had made a hundred times before, but for whatever reason, this time she went to the floor.

I want to be clear about Lianna Doty. This girl was on a whole other level when it came to her determination to do something. If there was ever a competition that required the best stamina, you had the average level, above average, elite group, and then there was a Doty level. That girl is the toughest girl I've ever met. When she went down, I didn't think much of it, I just assumed she was going to pop right back up. When she didn't, that was when I started to get a little worried. Doty was helped off the floor and practice continued on.

It wasn't until the next day that we gathered for a team meeting in the locker room before practice began. Coach P told us about Lianna's situation, and my heart sunk. Lianna had suffered a Lisfranc foot injury—a very serious injury that is actually very hard for athletes to come back from. Coach went on to tell us as soon as she met up with Doty after being carried off the court that day, Doty told her, with tear-filled eyes, "Don't you let me

158

feel sorry for myself." That's the type of teammate I want on my side. That's the type of teammate Doty is—she always puts the team first.

In an instant, our team was already going to look very different for the season. Losing Doty meant losing our starting point guard from the year prior. She had put in a lot of work, as always, in the offseason and was nearly averaging a three-to-one assist-to-turnover ratio during those early weeks of practices.

If I have learned anything from Coach P, it's that you cannot for one second feel sorry for yourself. You just have to roll up your sleeves and go to work. So that's what we did.

I was released to play on October 30, which would have been right at four weeks from my injury. I heard the Doc say "four weeks," and so that was exactly what I was going to make it be. I would ease into certain drills but wanted to get some playing time in the five-on-five drills since exhibition games were quickly approaching. It was a small victory to be back on the court, but it was also sad because of Doty's recent injury.

October 31 was a very emotional day for a lot of different reasons. My teammate Jordan Frericks had lost her brother-in-law to cancer and that was the day of his funeral. A few of us players and Coach P made the drive to Quincy, Illinois to support Jordan and her family. It was a hard day and we wanted to be there for Jordan the best we could.

Kayla drove us back to Columbia. Doty and I rode in the back seat and Kayla's roommate Cassidy was in the front. We had a lot of different and deep conversations on the ride home. When we were almost to Columbia, Doty said, "Mo, I just realized I won't ever get to play with you again." I told her how I had thought about that exact same thing just the other day but didn't want to say anything about it. Doty then got really emotional, which was a rarity for her. We continued the drive and let her just let it out. I put my arm around her, trying to console her the best way I knew how. I felt so terrible for her because I knew how hard she worked and how much she loved the game. I loved playing with her too, and so the thought of it not being a possibility was a hard reality to comprehend.

With tears still streaming down her face and her head rested on the middle console as I kept my arm on her shoulder, she muttered under her breath, "I want to do pitch action to help you break the three-point record." Doty was definitely really good at pitch-action and getting me open for a shot. It would be a major adjustment getting open looks. I assured Doty that she has so much value to the team in how she was already helping Carrie Shephard and Lindsey Cunningham, even if she herself can't physically do it. Doty's voice would be vital to our team this year. Her eyes watching from the sideline would be huge in helping us see and understand different things. She would be in a role she wasn't used to by being on the sideline, but she realized quickly that this was God's plan for her.

**Journal entry 10/31**

*"....Kay made a great point how Bri (Porter) said that it's so early that it's so hard to understand what God's plan is and why he would do something like this. One day we will all understand a little better. I strongly believe everything happens for a reason, even if I don't like it or understand it."*

\*\*\* \*\*\* \*\*\*

Looking back at my journals my senior year, I think

you would have thought I had the worst senior year in the history of senior years. I could tell I just put so much pressure on myself. Looking back, I wish I could have told myself to take a deep breath and enjoy the moment. There are a few entries that make me smile looking back at. Teammates lifted me up many times during my senior year when I needed it most.

## Journal entry 11/16

*We had a great practice today. It was very short since we have a game tomorrow. We brought great focus today and stayed locked in. Afterward, Jua, Carrie, and I were all taking ice baths and we got to talking about my shooting. I told them how throughout my career I have never strictly been a shooter. I did a little bit of everything. I got to the rim, handled the ball, and was a great passer. I still am good at those things. For a long time it has bothered me that I was a "shooter" because I did so much more than that in high school. I used to get upset when Mom, Dad, or Lauren would make comments after (college) games about how "It was nice to see you drive it, you can do that. Want to see more of that." I think it upset me because I felt like I wanted to be able to do those things with ease too but at this level it is much, much harder. Because I come in as a freshman a bit intimidated I hung my hat on what I knew I was great at and that was shooting. Coach P wanted me to shoot the ball and so that's what I was gonna do. Since my last year I have gained much more confidence in other areas of my game. I understand how to use my smarts to account for being a tad slower and a tad less athletic. I guess I just sometimes fear that I haven't become the best bball player I can be because I don't do the same things I did in high school. However, I think I really need to remember that I am*

*playing against future WNBA players and I <u>CAN</u> get
to the rim and FINISH. I <u>CAN</u> handle the ball. It is a
<u>mentality</u>. You could definitely say my career has been
nothing I could have ever imagined. But I think that
has been for the best. Here I am writing about how I
think I am an ok player but I am on track to break the
NCAA record for career 3 pointers. What?!?! Shep
and Jua were telling me (as we were ice bathing) how
they have played/seen good shooters but never anyone
like me. I just smiled and laughed. They were like "No,
but for real. You are your own breed." That means a
lot coming from them because they are both really good
players. So I am going to continue to do what I do. I
am going to knock down shots, handle the ball, get to
the paint and finish/dish. I am not just a shooter. I just
shoot the ball when I am open whether that is 3 feet
from the basket or 30.*

As you can tell from my post, I really struggled with
not feeling like I was the same type of player I was in
high school. I think I addressed it correctly in my entry
just when I talk about the level of competition I was up
against. However, being undersized, less strong, and less
athletic, were not excuses but things in which I had to
counteract and I did so with my basketball IQ.

I know I wrote that I didn't think that I had become
my best just because my game looked a little different
than it did in high school, but I can say now, a few years
out of playing, I gave my very best. I would put my drive,
determination, work ethic, and everything else up against
anyone because I really think I gave my all. Coach Porter
I think said it best when he explained how not everyone
really squeezes out all of the potential they have. He felt,
however, that I did just that—I had maximized my efforts
to be the best player I could be. That, of course, does not

mean I would play perfect or break records but for me today, I think it means that I can be at peace that I did my very best and invested all that I had into something I really loved. I ended up getting a whole lot out of the entire process, too.

*** *** ***

**A**s much as I didn't want to say that I cared about the NCAA record, I can't deny that it was something I would have loved to have accomplished. It weighed on me during my senior year heavier than I think I wanted to admit. But at the same time, I don't know that it was the record per se, but more that I wanted my senior year to be my *BEST* year. I think when you look at what your best year is in your career, you start to look at statistics. My senior year definitely wasn't my best statistically, and I think that is what started to weigh on me. What was hard to grasp in the moment was that teams were keying in on me with their defensive plans. People now knew who I was and it was on everyone's scouting reports that I was a shooter.

On top of all of that, I demand a lot of myself and I expect greatness every day. I flat out think I should make every shot. That is not realistic of course, but it was my expectation that if I was going to put out the energy to shoot it, I might as well make it. After my career was over, I was asked, "What was your best year as a player?" I responded, "Well, my sophomore year was probably the best year statistically, but I was the best all-around player my senior year." To this day I believe that. My stats may not have reflected it, but I was a much better player, leader, defender, and yes even a better shooter, even though the numbers don't reflect that.

### Journal entry 11/30

*It's just so frustrating when I visualize, try to think right thoughts, shoot lights out during shoot-around and warm-ups and then don't knock them down in a game. I won't lie, I badly want to break that NCAA record…but not at the expense of the team or driving myself crazy worrying about how many makes or misses I have!*

*It's hard to really pinpoint how I feel. I did every-thing I could to prepare. Maybe I truly didn't play in the moment. Too worried about getting out of a slump during the game maybe. IDK. I do know that I will keep working my ass off, be in the gym tomorrow, and watch film.*

### Journal entry 12/1

*A great day to get back in the groove of classes. I shot the ball great today on the gun and had a good film session with Coach Porter. Had a good talk with Coach P as I sat with Coach Porter to watch film. The biggest takeaway is to just trust my training. She also said how yeah it would be cool to break the record but 5, 10 years from now it won't be what I remember. She is so right! Any record that I hold now didn't happen because I set out to do that. I just simply wanted to do my best every single day. That is what I will continue to do and if it happens, it happens.*

I was very blessed to be surrounded by such great teammates and great coaches throughout my career. Coach P always gave me great insight because she was in our shoes at one point in her life. She was right about all of the records. The ones that I did break were not ones that I came in as a freshman and was like "Yeah I'm going to make more three-pointers than anyone in our program's history, make the most threes in a single game, and make the most threes in a single season." Those were never my goals, and looking back now, those records are not what I am most proud of. I am proud that I got to wear the words MIZZOU across my chest and represent my home state, my hometown, my family, my friends, and all who supported me throughout my life. What I take away from my experiences with college basketball is the amazing relationships that I developed with my teammates and with my coaches. That is what it is all about.

Doty also wrote me an awesome note. Keep in mind this girl wrote this to me after having suffered a season-ending injury. We would never get to play together again and that was a very harsh reality. Notes like these show the kind of impact she had on our team even when she could not physically help us. It speaks volumes about the kind of person she is.

> Mo!
> I just want to remind you what has gotten you to this point in your career and what people that have been on this journey with you see in you. You are flat out a tough player. You play fearless, you give everything you have in everything you do, you play in the present, you set great screens, you set up your cuts, you communicate on defense, you get on the floor for loose balls, you sprint your lane every possession, you always pick your teammates up, you close out under control, you get your hands up on defense, you take responsibility for your teammates, you give and take criticism the right way, you exhibit strength in your

*** *** ***

**I felt as though my minor** MCL sprain was a precursor for what was to unfold during my senior season. First, it was my MCL and then Doty's season-ending injury. I was finally fully rehabbed and back on the court with my teammates. I had to play in a brace, which I absolutely hated. It made me feel so much slower than I already was. I listened to my trainer and gradually would get out of a brace, into a smaller one, and eventually just wear a sleeve.

We were only a few games into the regular season and finally starting to find a little bit of a groove after losing Doty and me still trying to find my rhythm. Sophomore Kayla McDowell was really starting to shine. In our game against Colorado, we were struggling, but Kayla turned it on and got our team going. She was the spark we needed in our home game against the Buffaloes. Then, tragedy struck again. Kayla made a move to the basket, planted, and went down. I honestly didn't think it was anything major because she handled it so well. Then, through some small-talk with teammates on the bench, the word was they heard Kayla say the "F" word. Then I got a little worried because I rarely, if ever, heard that girl curse. She was helped off the court and later returned and sat on the bench, which gave me some encouragement that she was alright. Her performance helped boost us to a victory over Colorado that evening.

In the locker room after our team broke our huddle, I overheard Coach P ask Kayla what the doctor was thinking happened. Kayla said she was pretty certain she had torn her ACL. I think my shoulders instantly dropped. I couldn't believe it and especially when she was starting to really come into her own. Now our team had lost two starters from the previous season. I don't know what kind of injury bug our team had caught, but I warned everyone not to drink the water.

**Journal entry 12/12**

*What a comeback! So proud of our team! Down 12 at halftime but we found a way! Morgan Stock had clutch free-throws and Jua came in w/2:30 left and hit a 3, big FT's, and hustle plays. Biggest thing I'm thinkin about is Kayla. Most likely tore her ACL. She has worked so hard and I felt like things were really starting to click for her. She had a hell of a game tonight and even afterward, through her tears, she just wanted us to enjoy the win! I love that girl! She is so selfless and I just have to continue to trust that God has a great plan that we just can't see yet!*

Only eight days after tearing her ACL, I found this note card waiting in my locker before we left for our road trip to Wake Forest. I can't say enough how blessed I was with amazing, self-less teammates.

Mo,

I can't wait for you to ball out on Saturday. Keep shootin' lights out like you have been! You have been a great leader this season! BEAT WAKE !!

♡ Kay

**Kayla's note:**

We went on to defeat Wake Forest that road trip.

**Journal entry 12/20**

*...During Scotta's talk with us last night she brought up the graphic of me and the NCAA record and how many more 3's I need. I said how it could be easy to get caught up in that 'number' as opposed to the process. Si said, I don't think I've heard her talk about the record once." Jordan said, "She brings much more value than*

*her 3's." Lindz said, "She doesn't let a bad shooting night keep her from impacting the game." Their words meant so much to me! And I can honestly and confidently say that tonight's win felt so sweet even if I only hit 1 three! It was such a great TEAM win! That record really in retrospect, is just having my name printed somewhere with the title of something about shooting 3's. I value my relationships with my teammates so much more! I just want to play my ass off and take GREAT TEAM shots! Do my best and let God do the rest!!!*

"The Record" obviously was something that weighed on me. However, writing in my journal really helped me to reflect on the most important thing in my life and that truly was my teammates, our relationships, and the experiences I was having.

*** *** ***

About two weeks after Kayla suffered her ACL injury, it happened one more time. I remember we were on offense looking to score in the second half, so we were near our home bench. All of a sudden, I see Bri Porter go down and I hear the scream that too many people talk about coming along with tearing an ACL. It was a terrifying scream that I never want to hear again. It was Bri's fourth ACL injury in her career. It was amazing that she was still playing and doing great for us. I was near midcourt by our coaches' bench when she went down, I immediately squatted down and tears were coming fast. Coach Putnam was quick to grab me and the rest of our team and keep us locked in. A team like ours that had already faced so much adversity had to keep our composure, no matter how hard it was. Coach P went out to tend to Bri, who is also her niece. I can't begin to imagine the amount of heartache Bri and Coach P have been through, but they have continued to always carry themselves with poise and class.

We had not even reached conference play and we already had lost three players to season-ending injuries. These injuries only proved the strength that this team had within us. The adversity only made us lock arms tighter. Different people would have to step up and play their role. On top of losing three girls to season-ending injuries, we found out Carrie Shephard would also be finished for the season because of shin splints. This happened all before Christmas and the start of conference play.

**Journal entry 12/26**

*...My heart truly hurts for Doty, Kayla, Bri & Carrie. I will never get to play with them again. That is the hardest truth to face as a senior. It's easy to go down the road of "if only" but we don't have time for that! This is the only time Me and Bree have left. And yes, we have been punched square in the face with adversity but if Coach Phas taught me anything it is that, "You gotta roll up your sleeves and go to work. If it was easy, everyone would do it." God has special things in store for us* this *season! I'm ready to get back to work for my last season!*

Our team's makeup looked a little different coming back from Christmas break. There is no doubt that each team each year faces some type of adversity. It just really felt like this season in particular we got hit with a heavy dose of it. We accepted what we could not change and we got to work.

Mentally, I was ready to simply go to work for my teammates. I was finally ready to put my mind at ease with how I felt about the record for career threes. But first our team would take a loss that felt like more than just an "L" in the win/loss column.

## Journal entry 12/30

*Confused, angry, pissed off. I can't figure out
what we need to do as a team to get our "inards"
going. I had a bad feeling going into Missouri State
and maybe that was my fault for not saying anything.
I just tried to trust that all of my teammate's would
be prepared. I am in no way pointing fingers because
as a senior how do I shoot 2 of 12 from 3 pt line. That
is fucking bull shit. I am so tired of not just going out
and knocking down shot after shot, because that is
what I do. I understand I won't hit everything but I
gotta knock down open ones and stay in my shot.*

After the game, we sat there feeling terrible. Coach P
came in and took all the blame and said she didn't prepare us. I went back out and got her after that locker room
talk. We all told her right then and there that this was on
us and our effort will never be questioned again.

On the *LONG* bus trip back to Columbia, I went to
talk to Coach P at the front of the bus. I don't remember
how the entire conversation went, but it was just another
instance that I knew my coach just wanted the best for me.

*......When I saw Coach P getting emotional on
the bus talking about how bad she wants it for us!
How could you ask for a better Coach? She just wants
what is best for us and to give our best! To give effort.
Tonight was not a good night and we can't have
nights where we don't have effort. That flat out should
never happen.*

*I just want to play ball. I don't want to over think
things. The simplest advice I have ever received, I
think it was always Coach Norton who said it, "Do
your best, let God do the rest!"*

*No one gets to decide whether I break that record or not. I get to decide. I know how much work I have put in. I trust my training. I trust God has a plan. And from here on out there will be no more talk, writing, or anything about the record. I just want to play for my audience of One.*

And just like that, we dove right into SEC play. Our first game to ring in the new year was against the Tennessee Lady Vols — at Tennessee.

### Journal entry 1/1/15

*On the plane to TN & just reading through some of my journal entries. I read through an old note (a few index cards really) from Doty & I couldn't help but really feel power behind her words. After giving me so many compliments she said this, "**Your value to this team is huge and the cool thing is you don't have to be someone you aren't. You don't have to overthink things. You simply have to play the game you love with the passion you have and humbly lead the teammates you love with the courage you have.**"*

*I have learned to trust the process. But somehow I definitely have fear that my Senior year will be a disappointment. I don't want to just take the court and be like "well ok I trust the process, everything will be ok." Yes, it is trusting the process but it's taking the court with a determined and focused mindset. That is why Doty's words mean so much to me. She is right...I don't have to overthink things. I simply have to play the game I <u>love</u> with <u>passion</u>! If I can do that, then there is no way my Senior year can be a disappointment.*

171

*One more point I want to make. Yes, there is no doubt that I am proud of my records and achievements from previous years. And I get it when my Mom and others say, "Hey, the rest is gravy!" — Uncle B.C. I get what they mean and I should use it for my confidence. But at the same time, I am so <u>hungry</u> for more! Why would I hold myself back! I have worked way too hard. <u>Now</u> it is time to play with <u>passion</u> every single day!*

*** *** ***

I **was so very blessed** to play in both the Big 12 and the SEC as a player. I got to play against the best competition there is and also play in some really cool venues. I played against future WNBA and professional basketball players — not everyone can say that. As competitive as the season can get and how we can tend to get tunnel vision, I still tried to take in those really cool moments. I

I played against a lot of great players during my career, including Britney Griner from Baylor. She's a WNBA star now.

played in front of a sold-out arena in my very first game in the Big 12 at Baylor. Britney Griner, Odyssey Simms, and company took it to us that evening. I played in front of a noisy South Carolina crowd that painted a sea of highlighter-colored T-shirts that were passed out for a recruit they were trying to get — (side note, they got her. Her name is A'ja Wilson.) I played in front of a Texas A&M crowd whose student section was filled with rowdy Cadets there to support their team. I played in Tennessee's arena where the great Pat Summit paved the way for women's basketball. It was important that I take the time to really soak up those cool moments.

**Journal Entry 1/3/15**

*I had a moment tonight during Jordan's free-throws. I was behind J as she took her shots with the crowd booing loudly. I just took that moment in and thought how cool it was that we were playing at Tennessee in that environment. I always want to make sure I enjoy every moment of this journey!*

*I was just reading some more of the Bible and in Mark I really liked what Jesus said in verse 35: "Anyone who wants to be first must be the very last, and the servant of all." Is there anything more true than for me, as a leader on my team, to make sure I am always putting my teammates first & serving intentionally?*

A very impactful activity Dr. Scotta Morton did for our team was pair us with players from the Mizzou volleyball team that she works with, as well. Scotta had each of the volleyball girls write us letters — having an understanding of personalities and what we are all going through, she had a good idea of how to pair us up. Our Mizzou volleyball team had been experiencing quite a bit

173

of success and I knew a lot of the girls on the team who had come to Mizzou as freshmen with me. These letters were such a great idea and came at the perfect time of the season.

Morgan,

can you believe that it is already your last season? Take it from someone who is already finished at Mizzou, don't take any day for granted. I know that things aren't going the way yall planned, with team injuries and people having to play different positions, but it will get better. clearly my senior season didn't go as I had planned but I can honestly say I gave it everything I had and I think thats what matters most. Be the senior that leads by example, be the senior that everyone looks up to. No matter what the reason is, everyone should be playing for the person next to them, I'm saying this because I have been through seasons where I wish I would have done more, comanded more from people. Even this past season, at times I

## Journal Entry 1/29

*"...I also wanted to take note of personal letters that we all received from the volleyball girls. We got to read them yesterday and then we discussed them today before the game. Whitney Little wrote to me. The two things that stuck out most to me was she talked about how our season maybe isn't going as planned and with our injuries it's hard but things will get better. She said her senior year didn't go as planned but she could honestly say she gave it her all and that was really all that mattered. I just feel like I can really relate to that. My senior year hasn't been perfect and all sunshine and rainbows but I, and my team are still fighting like hell! Just waitin on those diamonds to fall!*

*The second thing Whitney's letter said was how sometimes being a leader she didn't always know what to say, or if she should say something. But she found that if she spoke with confidence, then it really didn't matter. I just thought about how Coach P told me it doesn't always necessarily matter what you are saying but say it with <u>passion</u> and so your teammates feel that!"*

It's kind of crazy reading back through my journals. You would think based solely on reading these that I had the worst senior season in the history of senior seasons. It was far from reality. Sure, I wasn't pleased with some of my numbers, and they weren't as astounding as I had produced in my sophomore and junior seasons.

The thing is, my senior season was a huge personal year of growth. I think having this journal my senior season was huge because I had a lot of emotions and by writing them out, it really allowed me to confront my emotions and get them out and just talk myself through them. Looking back now, I wish I could give senior year Mo advice and tell her to enjoy herself a little more and just play ball. Sometimes it is easier said than done when you are in it.

### Journal entry 2/12

*I should have stayed out on #33. Even though it was a scrambled play, I should have been there. I can't really put in words how I feel about this loss. As usual the last thing I feel like doing is writing about it. I have to do and be better for my team. I just have to.*

This was following a critical loss against Alabama on the road. We really needed this win in terms of keeping our NCAA tournament hopes alive. It was a game we had but lost in the final seconds. To this day I feel like I really could have grabbed the rebound, but I hesitated. The scrambled play ended with a kick-out to #33 for a made three-point shot. I didn't always cry after losses, but that one stung because I felt like it was really my fault and my dream of going dancing in the tournament was fading fast.

### Journal entry 2/14

*Today was a better day mentally for me. Having to watch Bama film was hard. I had watched that last defensive play about 10 times when I got home and then had to watch it in film the next day. My eyes watered in film as it played on the screen. How different things may have been if I had only snagged that rebound or got to the shooter quicker. I try not to blame myself but it's hard. Watching film I had a couple other soft box-outs and a blow-by. Not okay at all. I HATE being called soft…hate it! But like coach told*

*me, if we can channel this stuff in the right direction,*
*the hurt from that game can be good. I think for me*
*though, it's seeing that I blew my chance at a NCAA*
*tourney bid. It is what it is though and guess what, we*
*have the SEC tourney and we can just punch our own*
*damn ticket to the dance. I know at tomorrow's game I*
*will nail my box outs, I will explode to the ball, I will*
*lead my team. We play one way!*

My journal always helped me to bring my thoughts into a growth-mindset. Was I hurting? Yes. Would winning the SEC tournament be extremely hard to do? Yes. But that is what we are all playing for — championships. Whether you believe it can or can't be done, you are probably right. When we faced adversity, we did what Coach P always told us to do: "Roll up our sleeves and go to work."

***    ***    ***

**I think there has only** been two times in my career that winning a basketball game brought me to tears. The first was my junior year in high school when we beat Verona in the quarterfinals to advance to the final four for the first time in Montrose basketball history. The second was my senior season, and I wasn't even on the floor during the final seconds.

**Journal entry 2/26**

*I cannot even describe how proud I am of my*
*team! Maddie hit a 3 at the buzzer to beat A&M! We*
*broke their 17 home-game win streak! The arena was*
*packed but we kept our poise. Of course, I wish I could*
*have made a bigger impact on the game. But that does*
*not take away the excitement I have. I was in tears*

*after the game because I knew how important it was for us to get that win to keep our NCAA hopes alive and my team did that. I am so thankful! Maddie and Morgan played awesome and I am so happy for them. Their grandpa was definitely watching over tonight. Si, J, Linds, everyone really had such big minutes. I am just so happy. Now I want to get Arkansas on Sunday! One game at a time!*

As I watched from the bench, we ran the exact same play that we failed to execute against Alabama just games before. This time, the outcome was much sweeter. Sierra Michaelis drove the ball down the right sideline, she got deep to the right block, stride-stepped to a stop, turned behind and passed the ball to Maddie filling behind in the corner.

No sooner than the ball hit Maddie's hands it was off in the air and going swish through the net. The bench went nuts! I remember as we stormed the court celebrating, I got to Maddie and grabbed her face with both my hands and thanked her. What many people didn't know from that game was that Maddie and Morgan had just gotten word from home the night before that their grandfather had passed. It was an emotional time and after reflection, they both decided on game day that they still wanted to stay in College Station and play. Their granddad certainly was watching over them as they both played amazing. It was a really cool thing to be a part of.

### Journal entry 2/28

*Tomorrow is Senior Day. I cannot believe it is my turn to walk out on the court as a senior. It just seems unreal. Texting Coach last night about being ready for Arkansas. And I shared that I felt like at A&M I didn't contribute much so I am just ready to go out and compete again. Coach told me I opened up driving lanes because of the attention I drew and you can't measure focus, passion, and intensity in a stat line. Coach P always knows what to say to get my mind right. And knowing that she is going to be straight-forward and honest makes me feel good too.*

*I'm really hoping that the snow can hold off for a bit cuz I want everyone to be able to come to the game and do so safely!*

*Our team is in a great place. I can feel the focus at practice. We are ready for Arkansas. Ready to make it rain one more time in Mizzou Arena!*

I wish every athlete on the planet could understand those words spoken by my coach to me — "you can't measure focus, passion and intensity in a stat line." It is true we live in a world where the attention is going to go to the "star" of the game. Could you imagine a scoreboard at a game that kept stats of deflections, charges, hustle plays, or amount of communication instead of just points and rebounds? I think a lot of players would feel much more valued if there was more attention given to the "little things." After the A&M game, I felt that I didn't contribute much based on what my stat line showed. However, I prepared the best I could, gave my best focus and effort and those things simply don't show up to someone who did not watch the game. Coach P made me feel valued and made me realize I offer way more than scoring.

*** *** ***

**I** **remember many** Senior Days before mine. I always watched as the seniors walked out on the court with their families and waved to the crowd. Videos played on the

JumboTron highlighting their careers. My day finally had come and I wasn't sure at all how I would react. Would I laugh, cry, or both? Apparently, there were a lot of bets going around heavily favoring that I would be the one to cry.

Bree Fowler and I were the lone seniors. We came in as freshmen and now we would leave as seniors. When we were freshmen, Bree always joked how she could easily spot her parents in the crowd at Mizzou Arena. As the years went on, and we continued to build the program, it got harder and harder to locate her family. We always told each other that by the time we were seniors, the place would be packed. Well, the day came, and Mizzou Arena was not what you would call packed. However, it was a lot more full than that first game we played as little freshman, and it was still jam packed full of loyal fans, family, and friends who had been there for us since day one.

### Journal entry 3/1

*A great team win today! My team sent Bree and I out on a win The locker room looked great with all of the decorations and I loved reading what all my teammates wrote on my poster! Our team finished 7th in the SEC — we were picked to finish 12th and that was with a healthy roster! We face Georgia in the first round of the SEC tournament! I am so jacked for this tourney!*

*As far as the game today. I surprisingly didn't cry. The closest I came to crying was afterward in my car on the way to dinner just cuz I am beyond frustrated and pissed on how I shot and played. I was 2-8 and 0 rebounds. Just not pleased with my productivity the past 2 games. I want to do more for my team! And I will do more. I will continue to work hard every single day. Very cool memories that I have had on the Mizzou Arena floor and I will cherish them forever!*

Being able to look back and reflect on my senior day, it truly was special. I know I am harder on myself than anyone and that's why my journal entries often make it seem like I'm some scrub who has never played the game before — which is far from the truth. As the game wound down and was well in hand, Coach P made sure to give Bree and I recognition by subbing us out. As the horn sounded for my substitution, I ran over toward the scorer's table and Bree pointed in the air. We did our signature side bump, made famous our freshman year, one last time in Mizzou Arena. We made our way down the bench giving everyone hugs, meeting each other at the end and embracing one last time. The journey together at Mizzou sure was a hell of a ride and I would not have wanted anyone else by my side than Bree Fowler. We were one hell of a duo and I am forever grateful for our paths crossing. And by the way, Bree was the one to cry during our highlight video, not me. Everyone lost the bet on that one! Bree may look tough, but I also know her sensitive side. Love you Bree!

I spent a lot of hours in Mizzou Arena. I won a high school state championship on that floor, played my first ever Division I collegiate game, broke a single game record with 11 made threes, broke a single-season record with 112 three-pointers, broke a career record 367 made threes and joined the 1,000-point club.

I spent countless hours in the quiet gym shooting. I would go over missed shots and mistakes the day after the game to simulate the exact scenario and prove I could do it. I laughed on that court and I cried on that court. I doubted my ability on that court and then grew in my confidence and took that floor with swagger. That floor was really good to me for a lot of years. It holds a very special place in my heart. It's a place that will always feel like home. The old saying goes, "What makes a house a home? The people in it." My amazing coaches, team-mates, fans, and the community made Mizzou Arena home for me. To you all, I am forever grateful.

*** *** ***

**D**espite all of the adversity our team faced with injuries, we found a way. We were getting better each practice and just taking it one day at a time. With all of the struggles I seemed to have my senior year, there were still a lot of great times as well.

There's a fun story from our trip to Hawaii for a Thanksgiving tournament. Each Thanksgiving break we take a trip somewhere nice for a tournament. My fresh-man year, we went to Texas and sophomore year we went to Cancun, Mexico. Junior year was Miami, Flori-da. We like to joke that Lebron James had us over to his house, but we actually only really got a picture in front of his house ... on the outside of the gate. This was when LeBron took his talents to South Beach and was playing with the Miami Heat.

My senior season, we got to go Hawaii. What a dream come true! Coach P encouraged me to talk my parents into going. I had to do some very hard convincing. My parents' idea of a good and relaxing time is to sit at home on the couch, watch a good movie, have a few beverages, and maybe order Casey's pizza. A long time ago I vowed never to be as "boring" as my parents, but I have to admit the older I have gotten, I love being able to relax at home on the couch, watch a good movie, have some beverages, and order pizza (I guess my parents aren't boring. Or I am also boring). There is absolutely nothing wrong with that at all! My parents are simple folk and they rarely spend their money on things for themselves. They finally caved in and I think they will tell you they are glad they did. My

Aunt Vicki and Uncle Doug even made the trip as well.

But the most memorable part of the Hawaii trip did not come from the beautiful sites, activities, or even the games we played. It happened on our last day. We typically leave our hotel one hour and a half before game-time tip. Before each game we watch a highlight video to get us fired up for our game. Normally, we watch this video on the bus, but for this trip we would have to watch it together in one of the hotel rooms because the DVD player didn't work on our bus.

Okay, cool, no problem. It didn't really feel like that messed with our routine too much. Our team of 12 girls piled into Mike Donovan's room to watch the tape. As the tape ended, we all grabbed our bags and headed to the elevator. We packed all 12 of us into a single elevator—no big deal we do this all the time. We press the "L" button to head to the lobby. We can feel the elevator going down, down, down. As we reached what had to be the lobby, the elevator dropped just a tad bit more than what felt normal. The doors didn't open. We all looked at each other as if to say, "You have got to be kidding me."

As soon as the doors wouldn't open, a slight panic creeped in on some of my teammates. Kayla McDowell immediately ripped off her jersey—it was already getting super-hot in there. Other girls started to follow suit. We managed to open the first part of the elevator door, but it only revealed another layer. We started hitting the bell inside the elevator to warn someone that we were stuck. It seemed like forever before someone came and found us. We all tried using our phones to text our coaches, but no one could get a message to go through.

Meanwhile, the coaches were all sitting on the bus wondering where we were. Coach P later told me she thought, "I bet they are having a team pow-wow. That video must have really struck them and they are getting

ready to go battle." Coach Putnam had a different outlook. She thought, "I bet they're stuck in an elevator."

We all kept telling one another, we just need Coach
Page to come find us. Coach Page was our director of
basketball operations. She always had an answer for anything and everything. If only she would come back inside,
she would find us, and let Coach P know and then figure
out how to get us out.

Finally, we hear our coaches and we were relieved
they know where we were. We assured everyone that
we were fine but just very hot. Coach P came to the crack
of the elevator to talk with us. She asked if she could get
anything for us and so they managed to squeeze a couple of water bottles through the small opening, as well
as some ice chips for those who were hot, and then also
some Tylenol. Thirty minutes had passed by this point.
It would have been time for us to start our warm-ups for
the game. Coach Page was on the phone with the people
in charge of the tournament to explain our situation. The
people thought we were making this up. I sure wish we
were making this stuff up, but no. They tried to tell us if
we had at least five players who were not in the elevator
then they would have to play. Sorry, unfortunately we are
all on the elevator — we are a close-knit bunch.

We were ready to take things into our own hands.
Lianna Doty started looking around in the elevator.
With the first part of the elevator door being completely opened, it revealed a lot of the elevator's parts. Doty
could see what looked like a switch up at that top. She
swore it was the switch that would get the door to open.
The workers on the other side of the door kept telling us
not to put our hands up there though, for fear we might
hurt ourselves. Doty was being a little stubborn because
she knew what needed to be done. Part of me is thinking,
"Okay this girl is studying to be an engineer so she prob-

ably knows what she is talking about." Then the mother hen side of me is saying, "Let's not get hurt and just do as they say." Doty reluctantly listened to the orders from the workers. So time continued to pass. At about the 90-minute mark, we got the orders from the voice on the other side of the door to flip a certain switch up at the top of the door. Oh, you mean the switch that Doty was talking about 30 minutes prior to this conversation? Yes, that was precisely the switch. Doty was finally allowed to save the day. The doors flew open, we had to step up a good three feet to get out and we were unleashed like caged lions. We were ready to go to battle.

I wish I could say that we won the game that evening against California, but we came up short. It was a great game though, and against a very tough Cal team. Given the circumstances of being trapped in an elevator for 90 minutes, unable to sit or stretch, limited amounts of time for warm-ups before the game, and not to mention the mental toll something like that takes on you, I would say we did pretty well.

It's one of those memories I will never forget. When we were in that elevator, some girls were obviously more bothered than others. Some felt claustrophobic, others even cried a bit. But we were all there for each other. I think I even said out loud to the team, "I know this sucks right now, but we are going to look back and think this is hilarious."

We also did manage to get one selfie while we were trapped and even a little bit of video footage. It was an experience that taught us a lot about mental toughness and to be able to react and to respond to adversity that is unexpectedly thrown your way. We also learned never to try to fit the entire team on one elevator.

# 25

Chapter

**W**e **could not break** the curse of the SEC tournament and get our first win in the tournament since joining the SEC. All I can recall from this game was feeling absolutely miserable. You would've thought that I had no idea how to play basketball. I am not putting the entire loss on myself, as we all know that there it is never one person's fault nor is it one play that loses the game. My mental and physical struggle gained more weight after that game especially since now it was most certain we would not make the NCAA tournament, but would wait our fate for yet another WNIT bid. That loss was very tough for a few reasons. One, I wasn't enjoying the game of basketball. I could not find the passion that I had no matter how hard I tried to dig it out. Two, my dreams of going dancing in the NCAA tournament were crushed. Third, we had to sit on this game for over a week before we got to play another game.

We ended up bussing our way back to Columbia from the SEC tournament—a six-hour bus ride. Unfortunately, it allowed for ample amount of time to sulk and think about the loss. I also talked with Coach P. She told me she felt that the whole past month I seemed to have a "heaviness" on me. Our conversation eventually came down to "Okay, flush it and bow up … toughen up." That's honestly what I needed because I was so tired of playing mind games with myself. Coach told me to "let my hair down" this weekend and then be ready for practice in a few days.

I needed to give myself a mental break for sure. She

also told me, "This weekend I don't want you coming to the gym. Go for a nice run on Saturday and just clear your head." I did as I was told. Taking a day off from the gym was a rarity in my four years at Mizzou. It was something I needed though, and looking back I wish I would have taken more breaks as a player because it is easy to get consumed. One of my greatest strengths as a player was my mental toughness. My ability to lock in and focus is what helped me to be able to play at a high level.

However, sometimes my greatest strength could be my greatest weakness. If I let myself get overwhelmed mentally, I could easily slip down the wrong path. The mind is a crazy and powerful thing. It can help you do a lot of things you never thought you were capable of, but it can also bring you down if you feed it the wrong stuff too. For me, I was always so hard on myself and expected greatness in everything I did. Every shot I took, I expected it to go in. That is a great mindset to have but I also have to prepare my mind for how to handle it when the ball doesn't go in. Usually, I was pretty good at that, but other times when you become overwhelmed, it is a hard skill to master. Looking back and knowing the type of player I was, I do think I could have benefited from more mental breaks from the game to keep myself refreshed.

The bus ride home from the SEC tournament was very difficult. I felt guilty for the loss and I was also sad because that was the last SEC game of my career—not exactly how I wanted to go out. I cried for a lot of the ride. I got a text from Sierra Michaelis on the ride back. The text was a good reminder of my purpose for playing the game. I did not want to play for the attention or the accolades and recognition, but just to fully enjoy the moments I have left with my girls.

The text read the song lyrics: "I don't need my name in lights. I'm famous in my Father's eyes. Make no mistake He knows my name. I'm not living for applause, I'm already so adored! It's on His stage. He knows my name!" She followed it with, "Proud of you 30 ... love you more than anything!" I don't know if I have mentioned yet, but I love my teammates so much. They really are the reason the game is fun for me. They are a big reason why I push myself and invest so much because I never want to let them down. Teammates pick each other up and that's exactly what Si was doing. Those lyrics were really powerful to me and I used it as motivation for the remainder of my career.

According to my journal entry from March 8, 2015, the day I got home from the tournament, I received a tweet from Mizzou Prayer & Praise:

### Journal entry 3/8

*"Please pray @Mo_Eye30 will remember that her life is in God's hands and He has a wonderful plan for her!"*

I know God's timing is perfect in all that he does but sometimes he just hits you so square in the face, I just can't help but smile and say, "Good one, God." You sometimes just have to give God a wink and say, "I see what you did there." I got so many words of encouragement at a time that I really needed it.

The same night, I came across a photo on Instagram posted by WNBA star Candace Parker. What she said kind of became my motto. With her image the caption read: "And then all of a sudden, SHE changed. SHE came back a completely different person. With a new mindset, a new outlook, and a new soul. The GIRL that once cared about everyone and everything ... no longer cared at all." I remember thinking that is exactly how my mindset needs to be. It's like starting a new beginning. We would be heading into a full week of practice leading up to the WNIT tournament. It truly was a new season and I had a brand new fresh start.

The last piece of encouragement I got came from Kayla McDowell. She wrote me a letter on the bus but just got around to printing it so she could give it to me in person. Again, I tell you, my teammates are such a big reason for why I push myself so hard and also why I feel so bad when I feel I let them down. I was far beyond blessed to play with the group of girls that I did. Here is what Kayla wrote (And for those who don't know Kayla very well, she is quite the funny gal which you will see some of her

Hi Mo!
We are sitting on the bus and i just looked back and saw you through the seat crack (in the least creepy way possible) and got SO sad. I can tell that you have been crying and so I want to tell you a few things.

1. I am so proud of you. I am proud of your fight and your resiliency. You have not wavered for one moment. You have been such a great example of a consistent leader. I watch you (again, not in a creepy way) and you exemplify all of the qualities of a leader that I would choose to follow. You are easy to talk to, you work your butt of consistently, you know how to motivate people, you understand what it takes to be great, you are able to communicate efficiently, you are mentally and physically one of the toughest players I've ever gotten to watch, you have somehow found a near perfect balance between basketball and other aspects of your life, you are disciplined in every way, and you play with passion every day (rhymed). I can only hope that someday I will be able to lead like you do. Do not think that the little things you do that have made this team successful were a waste or have gone unnoticed. I recognize them and see them as equally valuable and pertinant to our success. Thank you for the example you set this year.

2. I understand (or at least recognize) your sadness/frustration and it is okay to feel that way. When you invest as much as you have it's going to SUCK! I know you wanted your senior year to go differently and there isn't much people can say to make you feel better. I wanted you to get that record, I wanted you to be first team... we all did. I think all the time "if anyone deserves it, it's mo." I am sorry those things did not happen. I know that you will always put the team before yourself and do not have an ounce of selfishness inside of you, but I also know the reality is that failing to reach the goals that you set for yourself sucks. If you want to cry/talk/laugh/sit in silence/eat food/ with anyone you know where to find me (:

3. I think you are the coolest person ever. Forget basketball, let's talk about YOU for a second. My admiration for the way you carry yourself has increased the longer I have been around you. You set an incredibly high standard for yourself and do not settle...EVER! I love that about you. You don't settle for mediocracy in any aspect of your life, whether it is boys, school, or basketball. Although people joke with you about having an impossibly high standard for the guys you date I think that is the coolest thing. You know what you want and won't ever sell yourself short. I love the confidence you carry yourself with and how you aren't afraid to do the right thing, even if it is the unpopular option. I am so thankful for your friendship and the way it has grown and I hope that in the next two years it will continue to grow (even if you are going to be the next Meg. G).
One song I have been listening to the past 3 months is called Give Me Faith by Elevation worship and there is a part i like so much that i might just tattoo it on my butt:

I may be weak, but your Spirit's strong in me
my flesh may fail, but my God you never will

To me it has just been such an amazing reminder that here on earth, I am going to get disappointed and sad, and things are not going to go how I wanted them to, but the one thing I can count on to always be there is God. I know He can never possibly disappoint me and He will never fail me. He doesn't promise things will go how WE planned but He does promise that He will never have to be alone in our weakness.

Thanks for being you. Love you,
-K

PS! I wrote this on the way home but am just now printing it. Thank you for keeping secrets and caring about Bri and I so much! I know that I can trust you and you want to do the right thing. You're the best (:

quirks in her letter):

**Journal entry 3/8**

*"Kayla wrote me this awesome letter. She is so sweet! I
text her how I felt like as a leader I feel like I should always have it together but sometimes I need to be picked
up. And that's what she did"*

Think about the lesson here. Sometimes when we
see a leader, we think they always have it together. Or
take a coach for example. When players look to a coach,
we think they have it all figured out and go about their
business with ease. Coaches are people, too. As a player,
when was the last time you asked your coach how they
were doing? Ask them how their family is doing? At practice you see your coach, he/she almost wears this armor
that keeps you from seeing what is going on because they
know they have to be in the moment for you in order to
get better in practice. You could go practice after practice
without knowing what your coach has going on with his/
her personal life because he/she is doing everything for
YOU!

A coach will invest so much time and energy into the
program because it is his/her passion. But sometimes …
just sometimes … that coach may need you to pick them
up, too. I think it is accurate to say I am a pretty independent person, but what I needed was a teammate to pick
me up, and that's exactly what they did. So keep that in
mind the next time your team's leader, or assistant coach
or even head coach, seems to be having a rough time.
Extend a hand. It may be a letter, a simple text, a conversation, or just a hug. Whatever it takes.

*** *** ***

That full week of practice with no idea where we

would land in the WNIT was grueling, mostly because each day I was making it so hard on myself. I was trying so hard to break through this barrier that seemed to be keeping me from being myself. I had a couple days of practice where I finally found a little bit of a rhythm with my shooting and so that was encouraging for me. The last practice for the week came on Friday before we would get the full weekend to recharge the batteries before finding out our fate on Monday. Coach P spoke with me after practice to see how I was doing. I always gave the same answer, "I'm good, Coach."

She wasn't buying it, not for a second. The thing about it though, was that I couldn't even put my finger on what was bothering me. I just wanted to enjoy the game again. Hopefully a couple days off before finding out our opponent would help me refocus.

It was no secret that I had been struggling to play well in recent games. I had met with Coach P a number of times and I would break down crying and not really able to explain why. I told her I understand that basketball comes to an end for us all and I didn't feel like that was what was bothering me. I think I was just becoming overwhelmed with emotion from not playing well and my season not going the way I had envisioned it going.

During that time leading up to the WNIT Tournament, a lot of things went on mentally, spiritually, and emotionally. First, I attended an FCA meeting because my teammates Kayla, Bri, and Doty were all presenting. Kayla, Bri, and Doty all suffered season-ending injuries.

### Journal entry 3/10

*I actually just got home from FCA. Kayla, Bri, & Doty were the guest speakers so some of us went to support them. They did an amazing job and so much of what they talked about resonated with me. A big thing*

Nathan hit on at the end was that we just witnessed joy by watching these 3. What they said and did was real. He challenged us that if we find ourselves lacking joy and we actually get to play in our season to turn to God and ask him to fill that spot. I definitely need to talk to God because I think I am having selfish feelings and it's just hard and I don't know what to do. I feel selfish that I even have bad feelings when I _get_ to play every day. Doty, Kay, & Bri don't even get that. I feel at times that I don't live up to the hype of what my senior year should be like and that I'm not as good a shooter as what I thought or what others thought. But, just like Doty said, she preached good words into her life…even if at the time she didn't feel them. She knew them to be true. Her rap tonight was awesome! That was the second time I got to hear it & it was that much more amazing.

I guess I just wish I could pin point exactly what it is that I am feeling. I want to gain that confidence/swag back in my shot and in my game. I want to play free. And all of these things are choices. I need to feed my mind the right thoughts and bust my butt every day cuz it's the only way I know.

I think I also wonder what God is wanting me to learn from feeling that I'm not helping the team or whatever. I feel like it has humbled me, just considering how I had all this attention my soph & jr year with my shooting and now I'm not doing great & at times not even in the game to help. I just don't want to steal myself of the joy I have when our team has that flow on the court. Doty talked about it tonight about how when all 5 work together. Sierra sent me these lyrics on the bus ride home from the tourney & I have since downloaded the song. It really hit home about my purpose for playing ball & not doing it for attention or the *accolades & recognition. I really want to enjoy every moment I have left with these girls & I don't want to rob myself of that joy because I played mind games with myself...*

Practices continued and I kept trying hard to work out of my funk. I had to keep a positive mindset and take everything one day at a time and really and truly enjoy the limited number of days I had left.

### Journal entry 3/15

*Had a good practice today. Still didn't feel like I shot well. I recall a good shot I had coming off a screen. It's amazing how I have only been remembering my misses lately. Maybe because I miss more than I make? IDK...all I know is I have to feed the good wolf. I tried not to get frustrated when I, again, was moved to the black team so Morgan (Stock) could get reps too. It reminds me of what I told my mom going into my Sophomore year. I knew we had guards coming in and I told my Mom I won't be outworked for my spot...the only way someone plays over me is if they can benefit the team at that time better than me. Morg has been shooting great...she deserves more time. Tomorrow is a new day and I'm gonna bring it at practice.*

*I recall hearing one of our highlight videos Mike (Donovan) was playing for recruits last week and it was a voice over of Eric Thomas and it's the one where someone is complaining about how they are working hard but not seeing results. Saying they have done everything that they have been told to do. They want to quit. ET says he can't explain it but keep working. That was something that hit me for sure! Stay the course. We will reap what we sow...*

The hardest thing I think that I was going through during my struggle to find my groove was knowing that I felt that I was hurting the team more than I was actually helping. I loved being the leader on the team. I loved being someone the team looked to when we were facing adversity. I loved being the one to grab my teammates into a tight huddle to refocus our group. I loved being the person who could knock down a clutch shot in a crucial moment. But what kind of leader would I be if I only tried to lead when things were going my way? Did it bother me that I wasn't helping my team and producing on the court? Absolutely. However, I knew that others were playing better and so my job was to be the best teammate I could be even if it was from the sideline. At the end of the day, I wanted what was best for the team. I continued to do what Coach P told me since the day I sat on her couch as a high school senior, trust the process.

### Journal entry 3/15

*We watched the Selection Show. It hurt to watch. It sucked seeing Arkansas get selected & celebrate. Just knowing I won't ever get the chance to go "dancing" as a player, stinks. It sucks watching them talk about Kaleena Masqueda-Lewis being 12 3's away from the NCAA record when I feel like that shoulda been me. I should have had that record & our team should have been waiting for our name to be called. I just read Coach Norton's FB status: "The measure of a person is how they respond to situations when they don't get their way. Persevere!" That smacked me square in the face! I believe what Coach P says and she has been saying for a long time that God has special things in store for our team and I believe it! We take on UNI on Thursday in the 1st round of the WNIT & I am so ready to play a game. Over my career I have had a lot*

195

*of ups, downs, and amazing learning experiences and
I believe those things have prepared me to lead my
team this post-season! One game at a time!*

\*\*\*  \*\*\*  \*\*\*

**We found out we were** headed to play Northern
Iowa in the first round of the WNIT tournament. I remember that game fairly well because I felt like for the
first time in a long time, I was enjoying playing the game.
I suppose my leisure run and break from the gym was
helping.

### Journal entry 3/19 12:00PM ish

*So I'm sitting in the hotel room and thinking
about how I need to make sure I'm ready to go for the
game tonight. I don't want to over-think things at
all. I want to play with a competitive edge & fire. It
is a brand-new season, brand new start. IDC what
happened the last game I played cuz I have learned
and grown from it. The most important thing for me
tonight is to play <u>present</u>. Be all-in, in the moment!
I want to tell Kay to be my voice and not let me "go
down that road"…We helped each other out earlier in
the year & I know having someone remind me to keep
perspective will help. I just have so many thoughts
about playing that I thought it would help to write
them down. I reflect on all of the years I have spent
playing ball…it is my dream to play for Mizzou. I am
living out my dream every single day! How could I
not play free & have fun today? And when I get on
a roll today…Do it again & again & again! ~I don't
need my name in lights, I'm famous in my Father's
eyes. Make no mistake, He knows my name~*

The day of the game we always have a little bit of downtime after our shootaround and before we have pregame meal. It was early in the afternoon when Coach P sent me a text asking if I had a second to stop by her room. She asked how I was doing and like I've mentioned, I got emotional. She told me, "You're really good at faking it. If we didn't have the relationship that we do, I wouldn't guess anything was wrong."

In some ways that was a good thing because I never wanted to be a distraction to the team in any way. I just wanted to be the leader I knew I could be. We talked about everything in my career. We talked about all that I had accomplished up to this point and who would have ever thought I would do that. I had tears in my eyes while explaining that I had no idea why I even had tears in my eyes. I just wanted to enjoy the game again. Coach P asked me to her room because she refused to let me end my career the way I was headed. She told me I was really good at "hiding it" but she knew me too well and knew she needed to say something to me because any game at this point could be my last. I had worked too hard and the game had given me too much to go out the way I was acting.

She was absolutely right, and I think just knowing that she cared that much really helped me. She didn't have to reach out to me to have a conversation but she did. She wanted the remaining games of my career to be ones that I loved and would cherish. We talked about how my mental preparation and focus was one of my greatest strengths and it allowed me to develop into the player I was today. However, sometimes I would overwhelm myself with trying to do everything right and to make sure I always did every mental preparation, that it was bogging me down. As I mentioned earlier, my greatest strength could also become one of my weaknesses by letting it overpower me.

Coach really opened my eyes by telling me that. It was like the weekend she told me to exhale and take a step back and I came back refreshed. Sometimes I just became so obsessive of trying to make sure I did everything so consistent because it had worked for me in the past but I ended up just completely overwhelming myself. By the end of our conversation, I felt so much better. Before I left, Coach P asked if she could pray for me. I responded, "Of course." We sat in the small living room area in the hotel room. Coach P sat on the couch and I rolled up a chair. She grabbed both my hands, we bowed our heads, and she prayed to God for me. In that moment, I had never felt so much love. It was a really special moment for me because it was just me, Coach P and God. To know that someone cared for me that much that they wanted to ask God to allow me to play free and be myself, I mean I felt pretty good knowing I not only had Coach P on my side, but God had my back, too. They have always had my back, but this was a simple reminder.

### Journal entry 3/19 3:35 PM

*...I feel so much better after talking and crying (lol) with Coach. It's like the 3rd time we have had a talk but I legitimately feel good. We prayed together before I left. There was something powerful about having someone pray to God for you. It felt really cool and I am just so happy Coach talked with me.*

*Now it is all about building my confidence. Confidence is a <u>choice</u>! Just talking with Bree, Jua, and Carrie earlier, they all think I'm a great shooter & that makes me feel awesome! I am a great shooter! I am deadly from anywhere & everywhere on the court! So pumped for our "championship game" comin up in a few hours!*

*Lastly, Coach talked about the great focus I have but maybe it has been so much that I need to ease up & I felt a feeling of relief when she said that. Thinking right is the ability to be free from overthinking. Tonight, I will bring <u>passion,</u> <u>energy,</u> <u>fight,</u> & <u>focus</u>! The perfect amount*

In games prior, I wasn't having any fun and it was mainly because I felt like I was hurting the team more than I was helping. That was the worst feeling I could ever have as a senior leader and someone who has invested a lot into the team — to feel like I was hurting our chances of being successful. It wasn't only that I felt that I couldn't get a shot to fall, but I was becoming a liability on defense and I would have a distant look in my eyes. I honestly didn't know what was wrong with me and it seemed the harder I fought it, the worse it got.

Maybe knowing that the end of my career was coming soon was what was wrong as much as I didn't want to admit it. I definitely didn't want to end my career disliking a game that has brought so much into my life. It was just really hard because I hadn't had that "feeling" in a long time. Anyone who has competed knows the feeling of being "in the zone." Nothing and no one can touch you. You feel free. Often after a performance like that you don't remember much about performing at all but you remember how you felt when you celebrated with your coaches and your teammates. I missed feeling invincible. I missed begging for the ball to be in my hands with hungry fingers so I could let it fly. I missed feeling that I was a good basketball player because I worked my tail off every single day to get where I was today.

That game against Northern Iowa, I was playing a lot freer. I wasn't thinking about whether I was hurting our team, but rather I was out there being a vocal leader again. I wasn't so caught up in my performance but more focused about what our team needed to do to get the win. Maybe that was the key, outward focus instead of so much inward and pressure. I still didn't have an amazing game by any means, but I felt like an integral part in the victory. I finished with 14 points and 5 rebounds, but I only shot 3-for-10 from the three-point line. I obviously was getting looks, but not knocking them down by my standards. Anyway, it was definitely a step in the right direction as we were fighting to survive to play another game.

### Journal entry 3/20

*Well we got the win last night. I finally had a little bit of fun out there! Really started to feel it again & it feels amazing! Coach texted me after & said she was so stinkin jacked for me and loved seeing that sparkle in my eyes again. This is only the beginning. We won that championship. We leave tomorrow for Manhattan for our "Championship Game" vs K-State!*

\*\*\*  \*\*\*  \*\*\*

**W**ith our victory over Northern Iowa, we advanced to the second round of the WNIT tournament. The way it works in the WNIT for hosting games is that each school puts in a silent bid to host. A lot of other factors are considered as well, such as the locations of the next opponent should you win, fan attendance, etc. We were hopeful we would get to host the second round since we had to travel to Northern Iowa for the first round. We always played so well in front of our home crowd—it really is an advantage. No such luck for us this time. We would be making a trip to Manhattan, Kansas to take on Kansas State. It would be an old Big 12 matchup.

There was no more bad blood considering there had been a lot of roster turnover since the last time we played them, which would have been my freshman year.

When I came in as a freshman, Coach P gave me a DVD with highlights of Kansas State's Britney Chambers. She was a phenomenal player and a really great shooter. She was the type of player that if you gave her any space, she was going to shoot it. Coach P gave me the DVD and said, "I want you to be a Britney Chambers for us." As I watched the DVD, I was thinking, "Okay, dang, she is really good." It was awesome to think Coach P thought I could step up and be an impactful player. But I had no aspirations to be Britney Chambers. I am going to be "Morgan Eye."

I actually had the opportunity to play against Britney when I was a freshman. I remember her being very good. It was a cool experience to get to play against her when she was someone who I watched film on. She was just recently inducted into K-State's women's basketball Hall of Fame.

The game against K-State was the one game of my career I will never forget. K-State played a zone that game. I think I speak for most shooters when I say I love when opponents play a zone because I am going to get a lot of shots. For the first time in weeks, I found my "zone." I caught fire mid-game and there was no turning back. I got one three to fall. Then another. Then a third. Okay, I'm feeling pretty good at this point. Give me four! K-State you sure you don't want to think about switching up the defense? My teammates knew I was feeling it and they kept swinging the ball to me in the zone. Five, six, seven! I think it was at about my eighth three-pointer, I was in front of our bench, I let the ball fly off my fingertips. As the ball continued to sail, I started back-pedaling, screaming at the top of my lungs and flexing knowing already

201

that it was money … Swish!

I finished the game with nine three-pointers, which tied a WNIT tournament record for most made in a tournament game. I remember running back on defense so

I always played with a lot of emotion and intensity on the court, and I loved being a good shooter. But there was more to my game than just shooting.

many times with a huge smile on my face and pointing and yelling with my teammates. I missed that feeling so much. Getting to celebrate with teammates for an awesome play was something that I longed for. Truly, the moments of making shots, which feels so great when you feel like you can't miss, but what you never forget is how your teammates make you feel when you are celebrating the shot.

On our way to the locker room, I met Coach P's eyes from down the hall, we ran toward one another and jumped in the air to side-bump. It was quite impressive considering she had heels on. We both headed to the media room to talk about the game. It was exciting to get to talk with the media about how as a freshman, Coach P gave me a DVD of K-State's Brittany Chambers and although she had graduated by then, it was interesting to see things come full circle and I being able to knock down those nine three-pointers. As Coach P and I stepped down from the podium, we headed down the hallway, her arm wrapped around my shoulder, "I'm proud of you, Mo."

**Journal entry 3/23**

*What a team win yesterday! So proud of our team. Thank you, God, that I finally played free! Hit 9 3's yesterday. I was so jacked! What made it the best was the smiles on my teammates' faces! I love these girls so much. I told them there is nothing I would rather be doing than playing basketball with them on Spring Break! Blessed to get to play another game. One game at a time! Thank you Lord for everything!*

There was a photo taken from the K-State game that has become one of my favorite pictures from my career. The photo is after knocking down one of my threes. I have my fists clenched by my side in a flex, mouth opened screaming with all teeth showing. It's one of my favorite pictures because I know what all went into that moment being possible for me.

I hadn't smiled that big in so long. It took Coach P constantly communicating with me and investing time and energy in me to make sure I could have a moment like that again. I am forever grateful to Coach P for a lot of things, but that Kansas State game really ranks up there because no matter what happened in the next game, whether we would advance and win the entire WNIT tournament, I got to have that feeling again of enjoying playing the game that I love with a group of girls that I love.

# 26
## Chapter

**We advanced to the** third round of the WNIT tournament and thought surely we would finally get to host a game. Again, no such luck. We went home, packed again, and made our way to Michigan. It was very frustrating for me as a senior not to get a home game, especially considering that any game could be my last.

I knew my family wouldn't be able to make the trip all the way to Ann Arbor, so it was extra motivation to try to win so hopefully the next round would be at home and my family could see me play. I didn't want my family to miss the last game of my basketball career.

The Michigan game was a battle. I was feeling good going into the game after the shooting game I had at K-State. The game began and I remember draining my first three and then a really deep three from the top of the key that had a friendly bounce and roll. I remember being really locked in defensively and just playing as hard as I could.

As the clock dwindled down and we fell behind, we had to start fouling and look to get some quick buckets. I could feel myself starting to let the thoughts creep in of it being my last time on the basketball court. Coach P must have sensed it because she looked me in the eyes and she said, "Stay in it!"

I had to immediately refocus and stay positive. It's never over until the last buzzer sounds. The game ended, and not in our favor. Tears immediately started to fall from my eyes. I had played my last game ever as a Mizzou Tiger. I think the best way to express how I felt after the game is to share my journal entry from that night:

### Journal entry 3/26

*"Just lost to Michigan. I don't really feel like writing but I think it's important to talk myself through some things. UNI, K-State, Michigan, there were times I thought: this could be my last shoot around, pre-game, etc. but I pushed those thoughts aside. I thought about the devastating feelings I could have after a loss but I pushed those aside and thought about the good feelings I could have. Scotta's tweet said it perfect. We may have bad thoughts but we choose which thoughts we entertain. I prepared my best for Michigan. I gave it my all tonight. Yes there were times I should have been lower on D & contained better & knocked down my open shots. I told the girls that no one game will ever define us. It has been*

Sometimes I just had to point the way after something good happened with one of my teammates. We were a tight group.

206

*an amazing ride. I love these girls so stinkin much
it hurts. I would do anything for them. It will be a
difficult adjustment not going to practice/workouts
or being around the girls…that will be the hardest.
I dread all of the free time I am going to have now…
LOL But really.*

I remember after our locker room talk and giving all
of my coaches and my teammates hugs, I just sat in my
locker for a second. Bree said, "Let me know when you
are ready." I put off taking my jersey off for a few minutes, but knew I had to do it. Once I got my tears to stop
for a time, I said, "Okay, Bree I'm ready." I mentioned
way earlier in my journey about how Bree and I became
best friends over the years. We shared a lot of firsts and
lasts together. We shared our first day on campus, first individual workout, first weightlifting workout, first conditioning workout, first official practice, first pregame meal,
first pregame chapel, first collegiate game, and many
more. Our senior year, we shared all of our lasts, and now
we were taking off our jerseys for the last time. We were
each other's rocks. We were there for each other through
the good times and the bad. She is probably the only
teammate of mine who has seen me at my absolute worst
and still loved me all the same. I couldn't have asked for a
better person to have by my side for my journey at Mizzou. Bree Fowler is my rock, my best friend.

I'm glad I shared my very last moment with her.

**Journal entry 3/26**

*"I asked Bree to take her jersey off with me to-
night. That was hard to do knowing I don't get to put
it on again. I would not change a single thing about
my journey. It has been one hell of a ride. I thank God
for this amazing, life-changing experience!"*

# 27
Chapter

**A**t the end of every season, we always have an end-of-year meeting with Coach P. It's mostly to reflect on the past season, talk about future aspirations for the upcoming year, and Coach P always asks us, "What can I do better for you?" Coach P understands that you can't coach kids in a "cookie-cutter" way. We are all different and that's part of what makes us great because of all the different and unique qualities we can bring to a team.

At the end of my freshman year, I headed up to Coach P's office for our meeting. She asked me what some of my goals were for the upcoming year and for my career. I talked about being more consistent and all of those things. I hesitated to say the next goal, but I learned not to hold back from chasing my dreams for fear of what others may say or think about me. I said, "You know the three-point shooting contest they do at the end of the year? I'd like to be in that." I was referring to the State Farm Slam Dunk and Three-Point Shootout, where the nation's best dunkers and three-point shooters get invited to as seniors. It sounded like a lofty goal just coming out of my freshman year, but it was something I always thought would be awesome to be a part of.

Following our loss to Michigan my senior year, I jetted home as fast as I could. I just needed to get away and be with family and not think about basketball because it was too painful. I recall getting a text from Coach P, checking in with me to see how I was doing. I responded that I was on my way home. She told me to enjoy and drive safe. I knew while I was at home the announcement for who would be invited to the three-point shootout would be announced over the weekend. I had so many emotions about it. It was something I just really wanted.

On Sunday afternoon, I got a call from Coach P. I assumed she was just routinely checking in on me to see how I was holding up after the Michigan loss. We had a short conversation and then she said her son, Blake, had something he wanted to tell me. Blake's voice came on the phone and he said, "Mo, you got invited to the three-point competition."

I was so happy in that moment. Coach P came back on the phone and I said, "Remember at the beginning of my sophomore year when I said I wanted to be in that competition?" It was crazy my dream was coming true. I also said, "Coach, I get to put my jersey on one more time." It's something that you don't think about every day when you take that jersey off for the last time that you won't get to wear it anymore. I was getting one more opportunity.

After finishing my conversation with Coach, I hustled upstairs to tell my family the news. We were all very excited, to say the least. We started researching who else got invited to participate as well. We couldn't believe this was actually happening for me.

I returned to Columbia and was starting preparations for going to Indianapolis, where the three-point contest would be held at Butler University. I was getting very overwhelmed with everything I needed to get done, such as travel arrangements, what to pack, etc. I didn't want to bother Coach P because I knew she always had a lot going on, so I tried to organize what I could on my own and, of course, with help from Coach Page.

Coach P had made a promise to Doty and I one day in the locker room that we were going to make the NCAA Tournament my senior year. Our program had continued to get better year by year and this year we were poised to make the jump from participating in the WNIT tournament to the big dance, the NCAA Tournament. What no one could have foreseen were all of the injuries and adversity we would face. That was the first and only time Coach P couldn't keep a promise. She knew how bad I wanted to "go dancing." But since that didn't happen, getting invited to the three-point competition was something extra special for me. I remember Coach P explaining, "Mo couldn't have the tournament, but this made everything right."

*** *** ***

**I** met a lot of really cool people at the competition. Everyone was very sweet and fun to get along with. The night before the competition, we got to go to the arena we would be playing in and shoot around a little bit. The look of Hinkle Fieldhouse is very historic. I personally loved the feel because it felt homey, for whatever reason. Some people had a few interviews to do and things like that. I later learned that Hinkle Fieldhouse was also the arena that the movie "Hoosiers" was shot in. This really made me feel everything was coming full circle with my high school team being related to "Hoosiers" because of how small our school was and then playing in Mizzou arena for the state title.

I hadn't seen the movie as a young kid, but since have, and now I was in the gym that it was filmed in. After Hinkle Fieldhouse, we got to have a little fun and hang out in the PS4 lounge. There was food and refreshments and also a PS4 tournament we were all about to participate in. Obviously, we would be playing the newest version of NBA 2K. I played Kevin Pangos of Gonzago and lost, but I gave him a good fight. Kevin had a com-

211

mitment, so I got to play in the second round by default against Pat Connaughton of Notre Dame, who now plays for the Milwaukee Bucks. I refocused my energy, thinking back to those days at Grandma's playing video games with Trevor, and I pulled out the upset. I advanced to the Final Four, which would be played at the after party the next evening. To wrap up the evening, we were all surprised with our very own PlayStation 4 and PS4 gear! I was very impressed with the gift. The last gaming system I had was the PS2, so I needed an upgrade.

The day of the competition finally arrived. We had a lot of time before the event later that evening, so we had the opportunity to visit a children's hospital. Those visits are always so impactful. The moment I can make any kid

It was an honor to put on my Missouri jersey one more time and compete on a national stage is the State Farm Three-Point Shootout. I didn't win, but I had the best score in the first round. It was fun.

smile makes my day and it's usually the kids that make me smile. There were tons of games to play and we got to hand out mini basketballs to the kids and take pictures. It was a special day for us players as well as the kids.

For the competition. I wore my gold Missouri jersey that evening for the last time ever. We got yet another free gift for participating. We all received the newest version of FitBit. We actually had to wear them throughout the competition for advertisement. I have to admit, I love my FitBit and wear it all the time now.

Prior to coming to Indy, I had already practiced back at Mizzou. Mike Scott helped me get the racks loaded with enough basketballs and we simulated the competition. I am sure glad I did practice, because it is a lot harder than it looks. You don't realize how fast you need to go. So practicing back at home helped me get a good feel for how to pace myself. I also knew which side of the rack I liked to be on and what it felt like to grab the ball from the rack because there is nothing game-like with that. I remember my first couple of practice rounds back home were not very good, but gradually I got better and better. I think the best I ever did practicing at Mizzou was 24 makes. I was hoping my preparation would help me in the rounds that would count the most once the competition got rolling.

In the first round, two people go at the same time one at each end of the court. I was kind of relieved not to be the first two to compete, but stuck in somewhere in the middle. My turn finally came up and I was ready to go. I remember taking my position on the right side of the ball rack. I gave my clammy hands a final rub on my shorts to get any unwanted sweat off—something I always had to do as a player before a game because I am a sweater (thanks Mom & Dad). As I grabbed each ball, I just kept reminding myself 'next shot, next shot,' trying to focus just one shot at a time, not rushing but not falling behind. If I ever felt myself losing my focus, I started singing the lyrics in my head that Sierra Michaelis had sent me on the bus trip home from the SEC tournament, "I don't need my name in lights, I'm famous in my Father's eyes. Make no mistake, He knows my name…" Those words just really helped to stay in the moment. At the end of the round, I finished with 21. I was the leader for the first round. I gave my Morgan Eye signature fist pump one last time.

The second round I didn't do as well. I only managed to make 14, which was one away from tying and two from advancing, and I was out of the competition. Although disappointed I didn't win it all, it was a dream come true to compete on a national stage.

The amount of support I received from Mizzou nation and loved ones from back home was overwhelming. It was crazy to see how many people had watched and were cheering me on. It meant the world to me to know that I had so much love and support from back home. My parents even made the trip to watch me one last time in person! I remember telling my Mom, "You know how you always would get nervous before all of my games and you said you wouldn't really miss that feeling? Well, you get to get nervous one last time." I'm sure she was shaking watching from the stands as I stepped up to the first rack to shoot. Coach Page also made the trip, which meant a lot that she would go out of her way to cheer me on.

One of the best texts I received was from Coach P. She texted me to say she was watching with tears in her eyes and that she was super proud of me. After our tough-love conversation, it felt good to hear that from her.

I headed to the locker room to change for the evening. I took a second. I Snapchatted a picture with my jersey on and captioned it, "Last time wearing this." Then I took my Mizzou jersey off for the last time. The rest of the evening involved just hanging out with the other players and a bunch of people involved with the entire competition. We also had the Final Four PS4 competition. I sadly did not bring home any hardware from the competition, but I think I earned some respect from the fellas at least and represented the girls well. The guy I lost to went on to win it all.

I returned to Kansas City the next day and headed home to Montrose for the remainder of the weekend before going back to Columbia for school. I called Coach P on my drive to check in with her. We got to catch up on everything that I got to do that weekend and talk about the amazing time I had. It felt good to have a conversation with Coach and know that we were good. I was excited to see her when I got back to school.

I forced myself to watch the reruns of the competition when I got home. It was hard to watch because I saw so many shots go in and then out. I just needed to make one or two to give myself a shot at the next round. It sucked to watch, but no one can rob me of the amazing experience I had. Any time people ask how I did in the competition I always reply, "I led the first round with 21! If we could have ended it after that round, then I won!"

### Journal entry 4/5

*Today is Sunday & I am back in Como ready for class tomorrow. I had an amazing time in Indy! My 1<sup>st</sup> round was awesome! I had the best score with 21. I got to do my fist pump one more time. I am disappointed with my 2<sup>nd</sup> round of 14. I made myself watch it on TV this weekend & it was just disappointing cuz I was 1 from tying and 2 from making it to the next round. But what a crazy cool experience! All of the girls were super sweet! My roomie, Cassandra Brown, won &*

*she beat Kevin Pangos of the guys...*

*Overall, a great weekend, with great people, great memories, & a once in a lifetime experience.*

*This weekend at home was also hard cuz I was thinking a lot about being completely done. People don't understand what it is like to be completely invested & then it be over just like that. It is going to be a process to talk myself through. And maybe I will pause & finally reflect on all that I have done.*

# 28
Chapter

**A**fter every season, we always have an end-of-year banquet. Each year it's a chance to thank the senior class for their hard work and dedication to the program. Year after year, I watched as teammates took their turn at the podium addressing family, friends, and fans about their experiences at Mizzou. Each year I could never help but imagine what my day would be like. That time had finally come — it was my turn to speak at the banquet and reflect on all that had transpired during my four years with my Tigers. Bree Fowler and I were the only two seniors. We came in together and now we were leaving together.

I can't lie. While I was writing my speech, I cried many times. I had good cause for concern that I would be crying when I delivered the speech, but only time would tell. Bree and I bounced a few ideas off of each other just to make sure we both were on the same page and not necessarily repeating the exact same stories.

With my first draft pretty much done, I decided to time it, and it was very long. I immediately texted Coach Page and asked, "So how long do Bree and I get for our speeches?" She responded, "Probably like 5-7 minutes." I was already at 15 minutes! It took that long to thank so many wonderful people who impacted my life during my four years.

When the night finally came, it didn't really matter how long the speech was. We all were in the moment and enjoying everything that went on. For this particular banquet, our team wanted to do something special for our coaches. Following Coach P's speech, Lianna Doty, Kayla McDowell, and Jordan Frericks took the mic. Doty went right up to our MC for the evening and said, "Brad, you are doing a great job, but we are going to take over for a minute." After that, we presented each one of our coaches with awards, included with a mini plastic trophy and certificate. Each award was something meaningful as well as funny.

I can't remember all of the awards but, for example, we presented Coach Page, our director of basketball operations, with the "SIRI Award" because she always knew the answer to any of our questions. After we gave out all the awards, we played a video that had voice-overs and quotes from each of the players. During my voice-over, I thanked my coaches for pushing me to be the best that I could be and inspiring me to want to coach so that I can impact lives—just like they did for me. I think our coaches were surprised and grateful that we took the time at the banquet to make sure they got the recognition they deserved. Our coaches always take a backseat when it comes to receiving recognition—they would rather give the credit to the players, but at this banquet we made sure they were recognized. My coaches are the hardest workers I know and they fully invest into the lives of each of their players and give their all to building our program.

So far, I hadn't shed a tear all night. I was feeling good—happy, not sad. The next part of the program was supposed to be a senior video that highlighted Bree and I, but there were some technical difficulties, so they jumped to the speeches, and Bree went first. She did great with her speech! She did such a great job of telling her story and thanking her family and all of our team and coaches. She only got choked up a little bit.

After Bree's speech, they got the video to work, so they decided to play it before I gave my speech. To this point I still had not "lost it," even having listened to Bree get emotional sharing her memories. The video started and it made me smile looking back at all of the old pictures and video footage from our careers. Then, out of nowhere, my parents' faces popped up on the screen and I absolutely lost it.

Mike Donovan, our video coordinator, had traveled to our hometowns to do in-person interviews with our parents in their homes. It was such a thoughtful gesture for him to go out of his way to do that for Bree and I. The video was a great, and I really got emotional.

I had to get up and talk right after watching that and getting all emotional. Doty introduced me before I spoke and, wow, does that girl have a way with words. She really did a great job and I can't say enough about the amazing woman she is. She truly is the epitome of what it means to be a selfless human-being, and I was honored that she introduced me at my senior banquet.

What's funny is while writing my speech, I never really got emotional when I wrote about thanking my family. They were the first people I wanted to thank in my speech, but I honestly hadn't written a whole lot. My family has always been there for me and I knew, while my time at Mizzou as a player was ending, my family wasn't going anywhere. I got up there and started my speech and as I begin to thank my family, I found myself struggling with tears. Having seen my parents up on the screen and talk about how cool of an experience it has been and what a fun ride it truly was, really got me emotional. I love my parents so much and they have supported me in everything that I have done. It truly was a fun ride and we enjoyed every second of it.

As I continued my speech, struggling to see through the tears in my eyes to make out the words on my paper, I thanked every one of my teammates and coaches. I made sure not to leave anyone out, because every person played an important part in my journey. I enjoyed sharing small stories of experiences with each of my teammates and coaches.

My speech revolved around the story I shared at the beginning of this book. I talked about the time I was a little girl and was going to be in my aunt and uncle's wedding. I cried at the thought of "being Cinderella." Fast forward many years later, and I am sitting in Mizzou's practice gym and Coach P nudges me and says, "Small town, huh? That would be a Cinderella story." I wanted the audience to know that I truly got to live out my Cinderella story. My senior year wasn't at all how I pictured it, and I never it made it to the "big dance" — the NCAA tournament. I never won a conference championship. However, I won so much more. I got to take away with me some amazing relationships, and that was what was most important to me. God's plan for me was way better than I could ever have dreamed up on my own. I concluded my speech by saying, "My Cinderella story has not come to an end. Now I just have to wear different shoes."

*** *** ***

**O**ne thing that somewhat lightened the blow by being done playing was knowing that I wasn't leaving my girls quite yet. I was offered the chance to be a graduate assistant coach at Missouri for two years, and I was thrilled to take it. It was nice to not have to leave Columbia, but my role would be completely different and my relationship with my teammates would look a lot different.

It really wasn't a tough choice to me to take the G.A. job, but it did take some thinking. I probably could have had a few opportunities to play professionally overseas, which meant I could have kept playing the game I love so much. But the small-town girl in me knew that I would have never enjoyed being so far away from home, especially now that my sister had Ren. I had just become an aunt, and I could have never imagined being so far away and not seeing that kid.

It made sense to me to follow that coaching path, because my coaches had always meant so much to me through the years and I liked the idea of doing the same thing for the girls I would coach. All the amazing coaches I had always pushed me and believed in me. That's what I wanted to do. I had just finished playing at a high level at Mizzou and, quite frankly, that was enough for me. I've had people ask me through the years if I ever regretted not at least trying it overseas, and I always say no, because I knew God had a plan for me, and this was it.

The banquet ended up lasting nearly three hours. It was crazy that it was that long, but I don't think anyone realized it because we all just enjoyed the celebration. Despite all the adversity we went through that year, we kept working hard and our team did things that, on paper, we probably shouldn't have been able to do considering the caliber of the league we play in.

This team showed what it meant to play with heart and to be selfless and to do what was in the best interest of the team. This group was very special to me and I will forever remember my senior season because of the amazing roller-coaster ride.

# 29
Chapter

**I** **don't think there** is ever a way to truly prepare yourself to be done playing a sport that you have loved all of your life. Sure, we can mentally and psychologically try to prepare, but nothing is like the true reality when it finally hits you. As a senior, I kept dreading the day that I would be walking out of class with no workout to go to. No practice, no weights, no film session. No reminder text if I am running late for a workout. No curfew. It doesn't really matter what I eat anymore — go for the burger and fries, and have some ice cream too! It doesn't sound like a bad gig at first, but I quickly missed having to "hold the rope" for my teammates. My team gave me purpose to what I did on a daily basis, and now that was gone. I think the day it really hit me that it was coming to an end was the night before my graduation.

I typically wasn't the type of player to go shoot at night. Occasionally I might, but usually I got my shooting done in the morning or early afternoon. The evening was for homework and then probably bedtime by 9 p.m. so I could do it all over again. This night was different though. I had already played my last basketball game, but graduating somehow solidified it. I hopped in my car and headed to Mizzou Arena. I wasn't able to shoot on the main court since it was all set up for other graduations, so I headed to the practice gym. There were people in there getting things set up, but I was able to shoot on one end of the court. I was definitely having a "moment." I took a seat in the chairs along the wall, my foot placed on the ball, thinking how these were the exact chairs I was sitting in when I was on my unofficial visit and Coach said, "Small town, huh? That would be a Cinderella story." I spent a lot of time in that gym. I had a lot of moments as a freshman where I would just walk in with awe that I was on the Missouri women's basketball team. After four years, it felt like it was home, but now I was done as a player. From then on, I would be on the sidelines watching my old teammates proudly, just like a mother hen does.

The day of my graduation was probably less emotional than that night before. I was definitely excited to be graduating. I had worked hard at being a good student and striving to get good grades. I remember when I was still in high school, I was petrified at the idea of succeeding in college classes. I had this preconceived idea that college was super hard and the classes would be impossible for me to learn and get good grades. It was quite the contrary. I am far from being a genius, or even considered "smart," but I do know how to apply myself. I got really good at time management, and that helped with preparing for tests in advance. I had to work hard in school, and if that meant I needed a tutor, I did not shy away from seeking one out. Calculus was by far my hardest class. It didn't help that I never took a pre-calculus class. I mean, what is a derivative anyway? I am almost certain I won't need it when I become a coach. Other than calculus, my capstone class was hard, but mainly because the professor was a stickler. I won't drop any names here, but he did hurt my grade considerably. No hard feelings. At the end of the day, I graduated with honors — Magna Cum Laude — and I am very proud of that.

It's become pretty popular to decorate the top of your graduation cap, so I joined in on the fun. I knew what I wanted it to say, but also knew my sister had all the artistic abilities in the family. She happily created a design with what I wanted the hat to say. Along the edges of the squared cap read: "Double Major: Marketing & 3 Point Shooting" and then in the middle, it said: 3ye #30. I thought it was fairly clever and fun. I got the idea of using the number 3 in my name from a graphic that was used when I was announced for the State Farm Three-Point Shootout.

When it was time to walk across the stage, I was honestly just so focused on not tripping that I didn't hear a word the announcer said. I handed my card with my full name on it so I could get announced. Keep in mind, I am focusing on not tripping, so I have no recollection of this, but my family reported to me afterward that the announcer says, "Morgan Anne Eye ... for three! Business Marketing. Magna Cum Laude." How awesome is that? The announcer simulated what the announcer at our games would say after I would hit a three-pointer. I only wish I could have actually heard it. I would have thrown up some threes with my hands or something.

It was a perfect day. I didn't trip, and this small-town girl got some graduation love at her big-time university.

*** *** ***

Coach P shared a really cool story with me from my senior season. She was talking to me one day about her weekend recruiting trips and how they went. When coaches are all together in those settings, the coaches always engage in small talk. She told me a number of SEC coaches would say to her, "Just out here trying to find a 'Morgan Eye.'"

I was floored when she told me that story. To know that I had that kind of respect from SEC coaches was amazing to me. To know they compare my capabilities to something they are searching for in a player is quite the compliment. It's also kind of funny too because they are all out there hunting at these AAU tournaments and I didn't play on an AAU team.

I also didn't have many Division I offers waiting for me. I didn't have my mailbox pouring over with letters from schools, I didn't have my voicemail full from coaches, I didn't even have one "official visit." But I am truly the lucky one when it came to the recruiting process. I got the one offer I really wanted—and my life has been forever impacted by that opportunity.

# 30
Chapter

**B**y far one of the hardest things I have done in my life—at least so far—was going from being a student-athlete to a graduate-assistant. I know God has blessed me beyond my understanding, so it makes me sound pretty spoiled that being a G.A. has been the most taxing thing in my life, but like I said, my story is honestly a story of blessings. Becoming a G.A. was also probably one of the most humbling experiences of my life. I went from being the headline in the newspaper to doing my old teammates' dirty laundry.

I mentioned at the beginning of this book that one of my purposes for writing about my experiences is to hopefully help other athletes who have—or are currently going through—the transition from being a student-athlete to the next stage of their lives. I absolutely have no direct perfect answer for making the transition easier, but hopefully by sharing some of my experiences, others will learn from mistakes I made and understand they aren't the only ones who are struggling.

When I came on my unofficial visit to Mizzou and sat on Coach P's couch with my parents, she told me I would become best friends with my teammates and maybe one day they would even be in my wedding. I thought that was a farfetched idea because I already had such close friends back home in Montrose. But man, she was right, because I became super close with all my teammates. They are now all my sisters for life. After I graduated and became a G.A., however, I could no longer be in that sister role anymore. I had to draw the line because I was now on "the coaching side" of things. The analogy I have for what it's like to be a G.A. with former teammates is it's like being in prison. That may sound a little silly, but let me explain. I see the girls every day, walking the halls, coming up to the office, at practice, maybe a little during weights — and all that's kind of like visiting hours. But that's all it ever is. I could see them every day, but I couldn't really be with them. It's like having a visitor in prison come talk to you through the glass; you can see them but you can't touch them. Once the visit is over, you go back to being alone. Trust me, I don't know the first thing about what it is like to be in prison and my real experience is far from that, but that was where I was mentally.

Coach P had always told me — and all of her players both past and present — that it truly is the relationships that will last. You will forget about the wins, losses and records, but you will never forget the memories you make with your teammates. Of course, I missed the feeling of taking the court on game day and knocking down a clutch three-pointer or two. But what I truly longed for was to be back in that locker room with my teammates. That place is like sacred ground, no judgment, just you being you with your teammates. It's a place where you literally will laugh about anything and everything just because you can. It's a place where you can all vent about how much you don't want to go do conditioning or laugh about how Coach was really on someone that day.

There is usually never one defining moment in the locker room, but it's just that special place where you get ready for practice with your sisters, take the court and give it all you got, and then know you are all going to end up right back in the same place again.

In my first couple of weeks as a G.A., I had just finished up a workout and was headed to clean up. I was on my phone and subconsciously went into the players' locker room. I got about five feet in and just started laughing at myself. I needed to take a right now instead of a left to head to the coaches' locker room. In all seriousness though, it truly is the relationships that last and all of those "little moments" you share with your teammates are what you will remember the most.

*** *** ***

A lot of people have asked me before what a graduate assistant actually does. I'm sure it varies from sport to sport and program to program, but the best explanation is that it's like being an intern. My day-to-day responsibilities could vary widely. I basically looked at it as I was here to make things easier on both the coaches and the players. I got a lot of good experience with Excel spreadsheets by updating the player's class schedules, updating apparel inventory, and organizing recruiting information. I did some hands-on things as far as creating and putting together booklets for recruiting, players' weightlifting manuals, camp booklets, etc. I only messed up punching the holes in the pages every now and then, in which case resulted in using more paper. I even managed to break the laminating machine one evening during summer camps that first year. But by year two, I became an expert.

Some of our busiest days were when we had official or unofficial visits with recruits. If those visits were in the fall, then most likely we were going to tailgate for the football game. When I was a player, I loved tailgates. What's not to love? You might have to scrimmage with the recruit on a Saturday, but then you got showered up, walked outside into the beautiful weather, enjoyed a free meal, and then attended the football game. As a G.A., things looked a little different. If it was an early kickoff, we most likely needed to be at the arena by 7 or 7:30 a.m.

For me, this meant I needed to be up by around 6 so that I could sneak in a quick run—running became my happy place when I was done playing basketball—and then get to the arena around 7 to start helping set up for the recruit. I set up tables, chairs, sometimes tents if we didn't have the big ones already set up, a television and speakers, tablecloths, centerpieces, bowls of candy, utensils, bowls, plates, etc. All of those things you enjoyed as a player when you were relaxing and enjoying the tailgate, now I was setting all that up. Even the smallest details I had so much more appreciation for, like the centerpieces on the table. Someone had to take the time to arrange each centerpiece with the perfect amount of dragon tears and flowers, and fill the vases with water.

Tailgating days for me was usually thinking "Okay, how fast can we get everyone out of this tailgate so that we can clean up and leave." Once the recruits left for the game, we cleaned up. Then we had the choice to watch the football game, but I usually didn't go because I was so exhausted. Typically, I chose to watch the game in our conference room and wait until the game was over to help with any others tasks that needed to be done before heading home. I regretfully admit that my school spirit was pretty low during the football season when we had recruits — but of course I didn't let that show in front of our recruits.

Another big responsibility I had was putting together "Save the Dates" invites and other recruiting graphics. I made the mistake when I first started out as a G.A. by saying that I had a little bit of Photoshop experience from high school. I was on yearbook staff, which still would have been four years earlier, and my expertise was probably nothing more than removing redeye and maybe cutting a person out of a photo. Nevertheless, I took responsibility and utilized my resources to try to get better with Photoshop. In the beginning, it most certainly was a love-hate relationship — mostly hate. I admit my work on the job early was nothing stellar. I hated getting asked to put together a graphic because I would put my best effort into it, only for it not to be used. It got to the point that at every staff meeting on Tuesday mornings I would sink lower and lower into my chair if something about a graphic got brought up. I would hold my breath hoping they wouldn't say my name but instead have one of the graphic experts at Mizzou do it. However, whenever called upon I did my best.

In order to get better and just to brush up on the basics, I was able to meet with Alina Rogers. Alina and I both came to Mizzou the same year. She played golf and was now working with graphics for our men's basketball team. She currently works with Utah men's basketball and she does some really great work. Anyway, she gave me the rundown of just some of the basics that I had completely forgotten since high school. She also set me up with all of the Mizzou fonts, logos, and signatures. Then I met with Ali Fisher, who essentially runs the show in graphics for all of Mizzou Athletics. She has done some amazing work and so I was able to just watch her do her thing on a Photoshop file. A big thing I took away from her was how you work in 'layers' in Photoshop and she told me to think of it as a cake with layers — which surprisingly had become very helpful.

By year two, I was putting together things that we used. Some of my proudest pieces were a simple fix to a group photo of our girls that covered the entire back wall of the film room. I put together the graphic of our team's core values to hang in the locker room as well. In retrospect, it is cool to think that as a senior on the team I was a part in creating and developing our core values and now as a G.A., I was literally making the graphic of those same values. I literally left my mark in the locker room. Each of the girls now have a graphic with a posed shot above their lockers. Whenever I made a graphic that I particularly think looks good, I always like to Snapchat it to my Mom and my sister. My Mom always asks, "Did you make that?" I laugh, "Yes, Mom that's why I'm sending it." I was so far from a professional, but it's been encouraging to hear people say, "You are really getting good at Photoshop."

Aside from office work, I also could be on the court for workouts to help out, which was  probably the best thing about the job, still feeling like you were a part of practice. We have a scout team each year that consists of about eight-to-ten guys who volunteer their time to play against our girls. I have always had so much respect for our scout team because they come voluntarily while getting nothing in return, put their egos aside, and challenge us girls to get better. On days when we were short a few guys, I would be able to step in and play. It's no joke how fast you can "lose it" when you don't play every day. It was pretty easy to get my shot back, but everything I did felt a step slower. My mind was thinking what I needed to do, but my body wasn't reacting. When you don't do your visualization every day and don't play every day, it all goes away really fast. It was as great reminder to me just how important all of my preparation and practice was all those years.

Through the weeks of being a G.A., I was adapting fairly well to my new role, but I had my weak days. I never really told anyone about them because I never wanted anyone to feel sorry for me. The last thing I wanted to do was be a distraction for no reason. The current team wasn't about me and how I was trying to adjust to not playing and being in a new position. I never wanted to tell any of my coaches, even though they had been in my position before, because I knew they needed to invest their time into our current players. They needed to give their attention to recruiting and preparing for the season.

As a result, a lot of days I went home crying and thinking about how lonely I felt. I didn't have teammates to go to the MATC with for dinner. I couldn't hit up a teammate to go catch a new movie and I didn't have anyone to just hang out with and laugh about nothing like I always did when I had a whole roster of friends I could text. It's inevitably a part of growing up and moving on. The only part that made my transition particularly hard was that I was still around all of my teammates, but just couldn't be with them.

Don't get me wrong, there were perks for still getting to be around the team and see my old teammates every day — not to mention still getting to play a part in building the program. I am sure Bree Fowler would say I was lucky, in a sense. She only got to see the girls every now and then when she would come to a game.

Sometimes I think it would have been easier to have just left Columbia, but I remember when I graduated how it was sad, but knowing I would still be around lightened the blow of being done playing. I knew it was an amazing opportunity, but it's just sometimes hard to remind yourself of that when you have an emotional and taxing day.

# 31
Chapter

The 2015-2016 season was well underway and we were heading to our annual Thanksgiving Tournament. The previous year as a senior, we went to Hawaii, but this year we were going to San Francisco. Although not as glamorous as Hawaii, this small-town girl had never been to San Francisco, so it was still an exciting trip for me. This was my first big trip as a G.A. It honestly was a little weird because I had a little more freedom. Typically, when we visit places, you have to limit how much you are on your feet or how much time you are in the sun because you don't want to wear yourself out for games. Now, for me, it was like it didn't really matter what I did. It was a weird feeling, to say the least. I think given the choice, I would have rather had restrictions and been able to be with teammates again, but I had crossed over to "the other side."

Road trips were always the hardest for me as a G.A. I spoke of the downtime we get, well that was when I felt the most alone. It left me too much time to think. Often times when I would get into my feelings I would just go work out for the second time of the day. This road trip was the first long trip of the year, so I think that is why it was particularly hard.

Our first opponent was Northeastern. We followed our typical routine of arriving about 90 minutes before tipoff. Some of the girls had taken the court while others continued getting taped. I dropped off some  bags near our bench for our trainer and as I was headed back to the locker room, I passed one of our players. My coaches were motioning for me to tell our player to fix her pants. We had a couple conversations earlier that someone needed to tell this player to fix her pants. She tucked her pants into her socks, and some felt it didn't look uniform and looked bad.

I could see my coaches motioning me to do it, but I simply didn't have the heart to say anything to her. I was not about to break the player's focus about how she looked when she was preparing to go play the game, especially when I didn't see anything wrong with how she wore her pants. Anyway, long story short, Coach P was upset with not only me but with all of the staff because no one had taken care of the "issue." I took it a little more personal because I was asked individually to do it, even though I really didn't feel comfortable doing it. I just remember feeling like crap after that encounter.

After warm-ups, we had our locker room talk and I stood in the back videotaping, like I typically do. When the girls left, I was picking up their pants and Coach P explained that she talked to all of the staff about the earlier situation and that it wasn't just on me, but on everyone because it was something she asked to have done. I totally understood and respected that. It was a small thing she asked to be taken care of and I should have just done it. I still got emotional and I assured her I wasn't just emotional from that silly situation, but more of an overflow of the entire trip. I just told Coach that "road trips are hard." They get lonely sometimes, especially when you know all of the bonding that can take place on road trips. Now it was just awkward a lot of the time. At dinner you usually sat elsewhere, when you got free time you don't really jump in with the girls, you no longer attended pregame meal or pregame chapel. It was all just very different. Coach P knew my transition was hard, because she had been through it herself. I was just really bad about ever sharing how I felt. That was a mini-moment of letting a little emotion go.

The next day we were set to play St. Mary's. It was late morning when the team was supposed to watch film for the game. I normally attended film sessions, but this day I wasn't feeling the greatest, both physically and emotionally. I didn't really want to go to film, so I decided just to stay in my room. No one would really even notice, right? I literally was about to fall asleep, which is very odd for me to get a nap in unless I'm sick or exhausted, and then my phone buzzed. It was Coach Putnam, "Hey, are you coming down for film?" Well, I guess I didn't have much of a choice anymore. I rolled out of bed and made my way into the film room.

As I entered through the doors, the girls sat with their chairs in a horseshoe shape. With their backs to the screen of the projector. I only assumed Coach P had some type of team-building exercise planned, which was nothing out of the ordinary. Coach P then stood up and said, "Mo,

Mo,

I admire you for a lot of reasons. First, as a basketball player and teammate, you were truly excellent, and I was inspired by your example. Now, though, I'm much more impressed by you as a person. The way you've so humbly moved from the spotlight to a position of serving in the background bespeaks the beauty and generosity of your heart, and it does not go unnoticed. I hope you never doubt the significance of your impact. You walk this earth so gracefully, and it has made an impression on me forever.

Abi

237

can you come sit right here." She pointed to a chair that faced the girls sitting in the horseshoe formation. I took my seat, wondering what was going on. Starting from the left, the girls one by one all read a hand-written letter that they had written for me. As soon as the first girl started reading, I mumbled, "Now, I'm gonna cry." I sure did cry. Those letters meant more to me than the girls will ever know. I struggled more than what appeared, or at least what I hope didn't appear obvious. After thanking the girls, I headed back to my seat. I looked Coach P right in

Mo,

Watching the way you have embraced such a servants role as a graduate assistant this year is such an inspiration to me. It takes genuine love and courage to serve the way you do. I can't thank you enough for all the encouragement, for rebounding for me, and most of all for being your honest, hard working, funny self. You never cease to brighten my day even when you may not be having the greatest day. I'm so so thankful for you Mo $!

Love you a ton!

~Lianna Doty

the eyes and said "thank you."

She only replied, "It wasn't my idea." I was a little surprised. I just assumed since I had a meltdown in front of her the night before that she probably told the girls they should do something to help me out. However, that was not the case. To this day, I do not know whose idea it was to write the letters, but the fact that they felt it was something they wanted to do made me feel amazing.

I don't know how they knew I especially needed that at that moment in time when I was really struggling with the transition. I kept the letters in my desk for the next two years as a G.A. I would always think of that memory of the girls' sharing their letters anytime I was feeling down about not being able to be friends with my girls. The words they wrote were real.

*** *** ***

**A hard thing to do** going from being a leader on the team to being on the sideline is the feeling of helplessness. When you see your team having struggles on the court, you want to be the leader to pull each of the girls' arms and rally them together and refocus them. As a G.A., that was no longer my role. As much as I wanted to be that voice to bring our team back together, it was not my job. I had to watch others step up in that position and take control—and we did have girls who did just that.

In my new role, I had to find a different way of adding value to the team. Sure, I was helping the coaches, but I really wanted to have my hand in something that would be directly impacting the game. I got my opportunity from Morgan Stock. Morgan was a senior during my first year as a G.A. Morgan and her twin sister, Maddie, were phenomenal three-point shooters and I had the privilege of playing with them for three years. Morgan came to me after struggling to find a good rhythm shooting in games and decided she wanted to shoot every day with me. To put together a useful shooting workout for Morgan, I first thought about all of the game situations that she was getting open looks to shoot. I watched film and even charted where she got her looks. After that, it was pretty simple. We simulated game-like situations and shot the ball. We continued this workout for the majority of her senior year and always made adjustments when we needed to if we had to add a game situation where she might have open looks to shoot.

When game time came, I took my position at the end of the bench to watch my girls play. When Morgan got an open look, I would grab Mike Scott's arm — he was the other G.A., who I just so happened to be dating. I grabbed Mike's arm and leaned as if to help direct the ball to go in. The ball would go swoosh, the bench would stand and clap, and I would nudge Mike and say with a smile, "We worked on that." I always felt like a proud mom on the sideline watching all of the girls play. I definitely wish I could have been out there playing, but knowing that I was able to play a small role in helping the girls was enough for the moment.

*** *** ***

It was a typical Sunday game day. The girls were still back in the locker room watching film of our opponent before they would take the court for shoot-around. Mike Scott and I already had everything set up, so I took a few half-court shots for fun. I always liked to shoot granny style (underarm technique) because I was actually pretty good at it. Mike always rebounded for me until I got my made shots.

The game that day was going to be on the SEC Network and one of the network's newest members doing some of the color commentating was the newly retired head coach of the Georgia Lady Bulldogs, Andy Landers. Coach Landers made his way where I was standing at center court. We got to chatting, just some small talk. Then he asked me what my plans were for the future. I told him I thought I was interested in being a coach at the college level. Mr. Landers spit some wisdom at me that day. He took on a more somber tone and got closer to my face, not breaking eye contact. He asked me, "What day is it?" I answered with a confused look, "It's Sunday." He responded, "That's right, and where are we?" I answered, "In a gym." He exclaimed, "Exactly! It is a Sunday and we are in a gym!" He began explaining to me the type of commitment that coaching takes. It was a Sunday and here we were, in a basketball gym. There aren't a lot of professions like coaching that require as much time and commitment than being a coach.

He used the example of a doctor. A doctor may do surgeries a number of days throughout the week and then could be on vacation. Of course, a doctor's job is very important and every doctor's hours may vary, but I got the point that Mr. Landers was making. He definitely made me think deeper about whether choosing coaching would be the best profession for myself. It would mean making a lot of sacrifices. When I am ready to have children, I won't always be able to make it to their games, school plays, and other activities. I will rarely have weekends that don't get filled up with recruiting, official and unofficial visits, and many other things that keep a program running.

I am very thankful for Mr. Landers speaking to me that day. He was someone who lived the lifestyle of a Division I coach and I very much respected his insights. I think about our conversation at Mizzou Arena every time I see him on the SEC Network. I have enjoyed seeing him evolve as an analyst on the network and seeing his passion come out when he speaks just like he did that day when preparing me for what life as a coach may be like.

*** *** ***

Our regular season came to an end. Yet again, we lost in the first round of the SEC Tournament. It is a wall we have yet to break through, but I knew this team would eventually do it. Despite a disappointing loss, we still accomplished a lot for the season. Our team finished 22-10 overall and 8-8 in the SEC. It was a very historic season for our program. For our program, it was the first 22-win campaign for the program since 2001 and only the second 22-win season in the last 32 years. That was pretty impressive.

We all felt pretty confident going into the NCAA Tournament selection show that we were going to hear our name called on that Monday night. We decided to have a watch party in our arena. Many family, friends and fans came out to watch the show. Our players sat in the front row, all wearing their matching tiger head shirts, and the coaches sat right behind them. The show started and the first set of teams were announced. Mizzou was not called. No worries, there were still three other regions to go. During commercial breaks, our master of ceremonies for the evening, Gary Link, entertained the crowd. He pulled a few players and coaches up for interviews. While the interviews were great, I think everyone remained nervous waiting for the show to get back on and to hear our team announced. The next region of 16 teams were announced, and still no Mizzou. The third region was announced, and still no Mizzou. The final region was about to be announced. This was our last opportunity. The girls all watched with their heads tilted high to watch the JumboTron. Some locked arms, while others held hands, and some were biting their nails.

As I sat behind them, I was even beginning to get nervous. I just kept thinking, "Our name has to get called. We had a great year." It came down to literally the very last spot called in the entire selection show, and there it flashed on the screen – "University of Missouri." Everyone jumped out of their seats with excitement. It was a special moment, one that we had all waited on for a very long time.

Once everyone left, we waited for Coach P to come up to the office. Mike Donovan, our video coordinator, was already downloading film of our next opponent. The coaches started researching and game-planning. I sat in the conference room to see if Coach P needed anything from me before heading home. She came up and you could tell she was happy and overwhelmed all at the same time. Before leaving, she asked me, "Are you good?" I think my automatic response to anyone when they ask if I am good, whether I am good or not, is, "Yeah, I'm fine" and I say so with a grin. I did that again.

But, in fact, I was not fine. I drove to my apartment having so many different feelings about that selection show. I should be happy. I was happy. Only, I wanted to be in that front row with my teammates waiting to hear that we were going dancing. I wanted to celebrate knowing that I was fulfilling a dream I have had for so long of going dancing in the NCAA Tournament. Instead, I was in the second row watching as everyone celebrated. I let the tears flow that night.

I felt even more awful for feeling the way I did. I felt so selfish for not just simply being genuinely happy for our team. Again though, I share these stories because I know they are human feelings and I am not the only one who experiences these types of moments. I didn't share with anyone at the time that I was struggling. I didn't want to steal the joy that everyone was feeling from seeing our name pop up on the screen. I let myself suffer in silence.

*** *** ***

We beat BYU in the first round for our first NCAA Tournament win since 2001. We would play the Texas Longhorns two nights later on a Monday night in the second round on their homecourt in Austin. I mentioned earlier how road trips were always kind of hard on me. When I had downtime, I almost didn't enjoy it because I felt so lonely. The NCAA Tournament was no exception. You watch as the girls get to experience playing in the biggest tournament in college basketball and you can't really do much but cheer them on.

We headed to our shoot-around on game day and I was really on the struggle bus mentally that day. I just remember that particular day being very bothered and sad about not playing. When we returned to the hotel, the girls came by to drop off their dirty clothes and grab some snacks since pregame meal wouldn't be for a few more hours. Our hotel room had a common area that became the "snack room." I was putting some of the dirty jerseys into the laundry bag when Bri Porter came to the doorway that lead to the bedroom. For those who do not know Bri Porter personally, I will say she is one of the most genuine and deep-thinking teammates I ever had the pleasure of playing with. I remember always telling her that I think I become smarter every time I talk to her. She is just such a sweet girl and her next actions speak true to that.

Bri asked, "Mo, are you alright? You didn't seem to have that sparkle about you today at shoot-around." I fought back the tears as best I could, but got misty-eyed as I replied, "Yeah I'm good. This whole thing is kind of hard, you know. I want to be playing." I further explained, "I have never wanted it to be noticeable or a distraction to you guys at all." That's what made me feel the worst — that a player of ours noticed I was into my feelings. The last thing I wanted was the players to be worried about me and my silly feelings when they should be concentrating on the game. I appreciated Bri's gesture more than she will ever know. In my experiences with Bri, I would consider her a fairly shy person, so for her to go out of her comfort zone to ask me to my face how I was doing, that speaks volumes to me.

I did what only I knew would help take my mind off things and that was to go work out again. Running and some lifting always made me feel better. It was kind of my safe haven, my getaway. When I returned to my room, Coach Page informed me that Bri dropped something off for me. I can only assume Bri was roommates with Kayla because I had two letters, one from Bri and one from Kayla.

This is why I played the game of basketball. These types of relationships don't just happen overnight. I get teary-eyed just re-reading these letters because I know it comes from a genuine place in these girls' hearts. I am forever blessed and grateful to have developed relationships with these girls who I can say I truly love and are forever my sisters. These are examples of the type of culture that Coach P has built at the University of Missouri.

Chapter

As emotional as my first year of being a G.A. was, it was also one of the biggest years of growth. I would say it was one of the toughest years, but it also brought someone unexpected into my life. Mizzou women's basketball typically has two graduate assistants on staff. While I was a senior, Meg Gee and former scout player Mike Scott were the G.A.'s. Upon graduating, I took Meg Gee's role after she finished her Master's program and moved to St. Louis for work. Mike Scott and I would now make up the duo as G.A.'s.

Mike was one of my favorite scout guys to play with and against. He was a scout guy for my first three years and then was a G.A. my senior year. I remember telling my teammates how he was one of the better scout guys because you could tell he had the ability to do some crazy things, but he always made sure to play realistic so as to challenge us and help us. He understood that his role was to help us girls get better — it wasn't about his ego as a male playing against females or feeling like he needed to show out. I think he always stood out to the girls on the team because he was such a sweet guy. And he couldn't sneak past anyone with those size 14 shoes laced so tight you would think they were painted on.

I first ran into Mike Scott in the Dobbs Dining Hall when I was a freshman. We were both standing in line to grab a tray of food. I recall talking about where he went to high school. I didn't remember at the time where it was, but I remember him saying it was a really nice school (I

247

later learned it was MICDS in St. Louis and have since been there and it looks like a college campus). I just remembered thinking, "This guy must be really smart to go to such a nice school." Our encounter at Dobbs was brief, but for whatever reason I still remember it to this day, and so does Mike. He remembers the interaction a little differently. He has since confided to me how nervous he always was to talk to any of us players. I find it really cute that he felt that way. I imagine while having that conversation in the lunch line that I was all chill and his heart was just pounding. It may not be true, but it makes him seem that much sweeter.

Obviously, I wasn't the only person to think Mike Scott was a really special guy because Coach P hired him as a G.A. I remember all of us girls thought it was a great idea and were really excited about it.

The very first time I thought I might have a thing for Mike Scott was on a game day when I was a senior on the team — I promise I was still focused — and we were loading the bus to leave for the game. Mike always stayed outside to load the bags one by one as everyone went to their seat on the bus — that job soon became mine in my second year as a G.A. I vaguely remembered looking out the window and thinking to myself, "He's kind of cute." I, of course, quickly shook it away because I needed to be locked in for the game.

After the season concluded and my basketball career had ended, I went through the stages of being sad, mad, happy, and repeat. I actually let myself be a college student for a while. I went out on week nights for the first time in my four years at Mizzou. One night a few of us girls went out, and we ran into Mike at a restaurant. We were all so shocked to see him because we didn't think he ever really went out. We all got to chatting and having a good time, and then there was this pretty girl that was around and I guess Mike may have had a thing for her (I'm not sure).

Anyway, my teammate, Maddie, decided to play matchmaker for Mike and started talking to the girl. Long story short, Mike got the digits and they hade a date set up a couple days later. For whatever reason, I remember standing there watching the event unfold before my eyes. I see Maddie standing there talking to the girl with Mike right beside. I remember thinking to myself, "Am I really feeling jealous right now?" Could that possibly be the feeling I was experiencing? That night was when I knew I had a thing for Mike, but I kept it to myself for a little while.

A couple days later, I got a Snapchat from Mike about which shirt to wear for his date. I was driving at the time so I couldn't really see the options, but I replied with, "The one on the right." He had asked Alex Wendell, one of our student managers, for her opinion, too. I think he went with her opinion, which was probably best. The date must not have gone great, because I don't think he hung out with her again.

When I had my graduation party back at home in Montrose, I made sure everyone knew they were invited, but didn't want anyone to feel obligated to come because it was a good little drive. Lianna Doty and Mike Scott both said they wanted to come, so they hopped in my car for the ride. Bree Fowler also made her way on the day of the party, which meant the world to me. This was Mike's first time in Montrose. I should've known then that he had to like me a little because who decides to ride along two hours to a small town for a graduation party? The night was so much fun getting to celebrate with all of my friends and family. It was nice to have a night to reflect on my accomplishments that my mother so proudly displayed in the house for our guests to look at.

As the night wound down, Bree Fowler was about to head out. Before leaving, she leaned in and whispered, "Do you like Mike Scott?" I smiled and said, "I'll walk you to your car." Bree said her goodbyes and I walked her out to her car. I told her how I wasn't for sure, but I think I may have a thing for Mike Scott. I told her about the little jealous feeling I had when he was talking to another girl and how I was taken aback by having those feeling. It was nice to finally be able to talk to someone about how I was feeling. Bree has always been a great friend to me and a great listener, and I was glad I was able to talk to her about how I was feeling.

After graduation, as grad assistants, Mike and I would share an office with Coach Jacob Linn, our strength and conditioning coach. We had a lot of fun together and a lot of good conversations that first year. Mike showed me the ropes during my first year since he was a seasoned veteran with a full year under his belt. He was always a good and patient teacher when it came to showing me how to do things. I remember him explaining even the smallest of details. "Make sure you walk down the halls in the morning to say hello to everyone. Before you leave, walk the halls again to see if anyone needs anything." You would have thought I was working with complete strangers that first week with this odd feeling I had. I had known all of my coaches for four years at this point but there was something different about being in the same offices with them and working for them instead of playing for them.

As the weeks went by, Mike and I started to hang out more and more. I didn't really have any friends I could hang out with because all of my friends were still on the team and there was that whole line that couldn't be crossed. My old teammate and bestie, Bree Fowler, was still in Columbia but she was typically busy with work so

I rarely got to see her. I also lived with a childhood friend, Kristin, but she always had work as well and had a boyfriend, which I totally understood. Mike was somewhat in the same boat. A lot of his friends from college had graduated and were moving on. He had a couple of friends still around, but part of growing up is that everyone gets busier with work and their everyday life.

Things started out very low-key. Mike and I would maybe do a workout together or drive together to Coach Putnam's house to hang out—all things innocent. What neither of us knew, was that each of us thought we "might kinda sorta like one another." One evening I told Mike I wanted to get Trops, which is a well-known place in Columbia that essentially makes alcoholic slushies. Mike had never been, and to me it was shocking because I have my punch card so I can get a dollar Trops after so many visits (I am dedicated and loyal). One day after work we made our way to Trops. Coach Putnam texted us about coming to her boy's baseball game, which we had been wanting to go watch. We knew however, we could not show up to the game with "the red straw." Anyone walking around Columbia with a red straw and plain white Styrofoam cup is a dead giveaway for having picked up a drink at Trops. We got creative and on our way stopped at a Chipotle to grab some black straws. We enjoyed the boys game and afterward went to Coach Putnam's house to watch the NBA Finals. Mike Donovan came by for some of the game as well. As soon as he saw the Styrofoam cup he says, "What the hell, Scotty (we had three Mikes on staff, so Mike Scott was Scotty to most people), I've been trying to get you to drink Trops for a year."

This was another clue that Mike must have a thing for me. Mike drove me home that evening and I fell right to sleep. I woke up to find a text from Mike reading something along the lines of wanting to ask me something. I responded that morning with, "Was this a liquid courage text?" He responded that it was. We finally had the conversation that I had talked to Bree at my party and told her I might like Mike Scott and Mike had talked to Alex Wendell that he might like Morgan Eye and so Bree and Alex talked and essentially it was public knowledge before either of us knew. The ice was finally broken.

*** *** ***

Ours was an unforeseen relationship, but one that makes so much sense now. There is a lot more to our story than just deciding to start dating after we both decided we liked one another. When Mike tells the story, he will probably mention how I "friend-zoned" him … hard! I can't deny it. We were slowly becoming a thing, but I had a lot of reservations about getting into a relationship. One, I didn't know if it was wise to date someone who I would be working with every day, let alone in the same office. I did not know if it would be something that Coach P would be a fan of, either. Two, I had not been in a serious relationship since high school and had only been on a handful of dates during my four years of college. I had very high expectations for who I dated. I didn't believe in wasting my time — or his time — with something that I did not see any potential with. Third, as much as I tried not to think about it, I think I had reservations about dating a black guy — did I mention Mike Scott is black? I had only gone on a couple of dates with a black guy before, but never anything like a serious relationship. I had to honestly ask myself if that was what was holding me back from letting myself open up to Mike. I was raised in a predominantly white Catholic community and while I am not racist, I still knew that being in an interracial relationship would be different.

As much as Mike and I tried to keep "us" a secret, there was really no hiding it. What was funny was that the coaches and players picked up on it separately. We had players asking, "Do the coaches know?" and Coach P was like, "Hey wait, do the girls know?" We always kept it 100 percent professional, even working just five feet apart. I think we had Coach P's approval because she knew we were both good people.

I think "different" is the best way to put it and I mean that in the sense more of how others were going to look at us than how Mike and I would look at one another. Bringing a black guy home to Montrose would be "different." Going home with Mike in St. Louis would be "different." I remember Coach P always telling me, "Different doesn't always mean bad." In this case, it definitely was not bad at all.

Our situation really reminded me of the story that Lisa and Michael Porter shared about their relationship (Lisa is white and Coach Porter is black). Lisa is Coach P's sister and is married to Michael Porter. They have eight kids, and half of them already have been on a Mizzou men's or women's basketball roster and Michael Porter Jr. is already in the NBA — but that's a whole other story for another day. I think I was a senior in college when I heard that Coach Porter and Lisa were going to share "their story" at a Fellowship of Christian Athletes (FCA) meeting. I knew I wanted to attend that evening so I could hear about how they met and grew in both their love and faith. A big part of their story that stood out to me was when Lisa started talking about when she first met Coach Porter. It was really cute to hear how they bumped into one another and so forth. Lisa continued addressing the crowd and encouraged everyone that when you pray to God to be specific about what you are praying for — she was speaking specifically about praying for what you want in a partner.

She continued by telling us her conversation with God. She said to God with a giggle, "But I didn't order black." I don't know that Lisa or Coach Porter envisioned themselves in an interracial relationship but it has worked out great. That story stuck out to me so much because I started to think about what I would pray for in a man. I would ask God every night to send me a man who is loving, caring, kind, genuine, someone who I am attracted to, has a sense of humor, MUST get my sense of humor (a MUST), respects me, etc. I didn't say anything about the color of his skin and it has never been an issue to me. I think it was just an image that I had always built up in my head that I was going to end up with a small-town, country, Ryan Gosling-type of man. What I could not see from the start was that God was answering my prayers. In fact, he sent me someone with more great qualities than I even listed in my prayers. I was just a little too ignorant to notice right away. Just because Mike hadn't fit the image that I had built up in my head for years, did not mean that he wasn't the one for me.

I think just hearing Lisa and Coach Porter's story made me more confident in being in an interracial relationship. It wasn't just me who had reservations, but Mike also had concerns about me and had never seriously dated a white girl. For us, the Porters were — and continue to be — great role models for us with their marriage and by having raised eight kids. I admire them for the challenges that they faced for choosing to be in an interracial relationship and know they will be great mentors in helping us in any of life's challenges.

Mike and I would have our share of fights as we finally became an "official" couple. Most of our fights were about communication, and guess how we resolved those fights? We communicated. It took a lot for me to get used to being in a relationship when I was so used to being so independent. When I was a student-athlete, I honestly could not have been a good girlfriend. I was too selfish with my time. My day revolved around basketball, school, and basketball. I got up early, worked my butt off during the day, and was ready to go to bed early to do it all over again. Sure, I loved the idea of having a boyfriend come support me at my games and sit with my family and then grab dinner afterward. However, it was not realistic. I could not give the attention, love, affection, and work that it requires to be in a relationship. Mike made a comment once about wishing he dated me sooner when I still played. I just responded, "No, you don't." It never would have worked because I wouldn't have been able to give him the attention he deserved.

I definitely believe that God's timing is perfect. I was patient in finding someone who I loved, and God blessed me at just the right time in my life. I was done playing basketball and ready for the next chapter of my life.

In this chapter, God was ready to place Mike in it. On September 6, 2015, I finally said yes when Mike asked me to "be his girl." Most people who know us would say we were together much longer—and they are probably right—but this was when I finally put my guard down and let myself fall.

# 33
Chapter

**O**verall, **my second year** as a graduate assistant was much easier mentally than that first year. The first year was a really tough adjustment for me. In the second year, I knew what to expect, I had been through it, and could be more focused on helping the team—but that's not to say I didn't still have my rough times. They just didn't happen as often. I will always miss playing and being with my teammates, but I really started to feel that I was growing up and maturing. I was ready to continue on with the next chapter of my life and felt that mentally I had made it through the fire.

The new challenge in my second year was being in a long-distance relationship. Mike had accepted an assistant coaching position at the University of Alabama at Birmingham (UAB) for the women's program. The head coach, Randy Norton, was my former coach at Mizzou, and he gave Mike his first coaching opportunity. Mike had developed a good relationship with Coach Norton during his time as a scout guy, so it really is a small world.

Regardless of distance, Mike and I made things work. Luckily, being in the SEC meant traveling to a lot of locations that were near Birmingham and we played on different days than Mike's team, so he was able to make the trip to some away games to see me. He definitely did the majority of the traveling when it came to seeing each other, and I owe him big-time for that.

Even though my second year went a lot smoother, I still have a few notable experiences that I remember impacting me during that time and have carried over into shaping me into who I am today.

*** *** ***

As our team was preparing to take on Saint Louis University, we gathered in our meeting room to watch film before heading to shoot-around. Typically, by this time we have already watched the scout film a couple of times, so the last session consisted of watching game film of a recent game or a game we played against that opponent. It just so happened that the last time we had played SLU was my senior season—approximately two years ago. I walked into the room and took my typical seat toward the back. The film screen was set up at the front of the room with the players' chairs creating a U-shape around the screen. The coaches always took their seats behind the players and the coach in charge of the scouting report sat by the projector right behind the girls and talked through the action. The tape started to roll and, as I typically do if it is ever a game that I played in, I begin critiquing myself. I like the way I start out. You can tell I am in a low defensive stance, pointing, talking, communicating with my teammates. As we transition to offense, I am moving well without the ball and setting good screens. The defense is on me tight because they know I am a shooter. A couple possessions later, I have the ball at the right wing. I make a silly dribble move into two defenders at the right elbow and lose the ball, and I quickly got subbed for. Oh no! I rarely get to see film with me in it at all, and now I am going to be left with that in my mind?

The film kept rolling of the game. I keep thinking, "Please put me back in, please put me back in." Finally, I return to the game and we are still watching game flow. I watch myself again. I like how my defense looks. I am on the balls of my feet bouncing around and ready to react. I am thinking "Okay, if we end film now I am satisfied with ending on something positive." Coach Putnam asks Coach P, "Are you ready to watch some of SLU's game against Georgia?" Coach P responds, "No, just a little bit more." A few possessions later, we are attacking to score, I get a pass and the shot goes up. Coach P says, "There it is!" The shot clanked just a little strong. She said, "Oh, I thought that was the one that went in. You (meaning me), get hot here in a second." I giggled and said, "Is that why we are still watching film?" She kind of smiles and nods, the girls all giggle. Sure enough, on the very next possession, I get the same look and SWISH, nothing but net!

Coach P says, "Had to end on a good note." I shot back with a "let it rain!" These were the kind of moments that remind me how blessed I am to work for such an amazing lady. She didn't have to keep watching film, but I think she knew deep down how much that would mean to me. She also probably knew I could not help but critique my every move as we were watching film. It was a cool moment for me and a moment that rejuvenated me and made me want to be better for our team.

*** *** ***

**W**e were at Vanderbilt University's practice gym waiting for the main court to open up. A few of the girls' parents made the trip to Nashville and got to come to watch the practice. Our coaches were walking through the scouting report with our girls for about 40 minutes and then we moved to the main floor. I went and grabbed all of the pennies with numbers on them that the girls were wearing and carried them to the arena. As we entered the gym, the music got bumping and the girls started their typical warmup practice routine. I stood on the sideline folding the pennies to put them away for shoot-around the following day.

As I was folding them, an arm came around my shoulder. It was Jordan Chavis's (JoJo) dad. He spoke close to my ear, and very softly. He said, "You know how JoJo had that really good game a while ago? I asked her what she had been doing. She said she was in the gym with Mo. So I told her 'STAY IN THE GYM WITH MORGAN!' Get her (JoJo) to shoot 1,500 or 1,000 jump shots every week!"

I smiled at him and said, "I can do that." It meant a lot to me that he and JoJo felt that I had a positive impact on the good game she had. I remember after she had a nice game that I texted my mom and my boyfriend that I had been in the gym with her those days beforehand, so I liked to think I had a small role in her success.

Of course I was only joking, but those types of moments made me feel like I have a purpose. I would never want recognition for it, but man it feels great to have a player — and even her parent — come up and say nice things to you.

On the same road trip at Vandy, I got a text from JoJo, "I just wanted to say thank you MO for shooting with me and helping me get better with my shot. … I really appreciate all that u do."

That kind of stuff makes me know that I am where I am supposed to be and doing what God needs me to do.

*** *** ***

The 2016-2017 banquet was interesting for me. I had a lot of different emotions after that banquet. This was my original post for my book that I wrote following the day of the banquet:

**Journal entry 4/18/17**

*Last night was our 2016-2017 awards banquet. It's always a night full of emotions as we can finally sit back and reflect on the entirety of the season and honor the work that our seniors have put in over the years. I remember how much I enjoyed my senior banquet just a couple years prior and I will always cherish it. This banquet we would be honoring senior Sierra Michaelis, 5th year senior Lianna Doty, and 5th year senior Lindsey Cunningham. I had the honor of being teammates with Doty and Lindsey for 3 years and Sierra for 2 years. I have so many memories with these girls that I will cherish forever and I think that was what added emotion to the night. There were many tears shed this night because of all the great memories but also the reality of it all coming to an end. Coach P showed the most emotion at this particular banquet than I have ever seen. She even choked back a few tears while speaking of the seniors. She always does an amazing job recognizing all that the senior class contributes to the program.*

I sat back and listened to all of the stories being told. Some were stories I remembered because I was a part of or had heard them when I was a teammate. Some stories were brand new as I was no longer in the locker room but in an office as a graduate assistant.

I went home from the banquet with a weird feeling—a sad feeling, I think. I couldn't understand or put into words what I was feeling but it definitely wasn't a happy feeling. I even found myself with tears in my eyes. I felt somewhat empty. But why? This banquet wasn't about me. It wasn't about my playing days or the memories I made with them when I was a player. It was about them reflecting back on their journey and the memories they made.

The best clarity or most sense I could make of the whole ordeal came to me the next day when I tried to talk myself through my emotions. I got up at 6:30 a.m. and headed to the rec for my morning swim workout. (I was swimming instead of running because of a little Achilles injury and, trust me, I prefer land over water.) I sat in the sauna after finishing my swim and talked through what I was feeling. Bottom line, I really missed being a part of the team. I missed sharing stories, laughs, and tears with my best friends. I missed being in the locker room every day joking and laughing about absolutely NOTHING!

As each senior took their turn sharing stories, I couldn't help but reminisce to when I was a teammate of theirs and think about how much they had grown since I was there with them. Now of course I have never left. I've still been here as a G.A. but I think that is what has made it harder. Do the girls even remember when we were teammates? I mean, I see them every day, but it's not like we can have the same friendship because I am now on the coaching side. I feel like I have lost time with them and it's hard to pick up a friendship right where we left off when our relationship had to turn to a professional one because of my role.

Coach P showed tons of emotions as she listed the qualities of each senior. She spoke about the love she had for each girl and the value they brought to the program. It made me miss my player-coach relationship with Coach P Don't get me wrong, I have a great relationship with Coach P, but I couldn't help but think that I should've done more to have a stronger relationship with her when I was a player. I know I didn't come up to the office near-ly enough as a player. I also had a feeling of envy as I learned that each of our coaches had shared "their story" to the team a couple of years ago as I was in my first year as a grad assistant and was unable to sit in on the meeting. I think it had to be one of the most impactful meetings as the players got to see a different and more vulnerable side to the coaches. However, I wasn't at the meeting and I therefore didn't know all of my coaches' life stories. Part of that was on me, maybe I just needed to ask. But I found myself wishing I had done more to develop more meaningful relationships with my coaches. I wish I would have shown my coaches just how much I loved them and appreciated everything they did for me. The truth is, I still have the opportunity to learn about my coaches as I work alongside them each day. I love them dearly and am blessed to get to work with them every single day.

I don't share these feelings for sympathy. I don't want to admit to anyone that I had these feelings because it makes me feel awful. I feel selfish enough just writing these feelings down on a page. The reason I do it, because these are human feelings and I know there are tons of other former athletes out there who have the same type of feelings, too. It's hard to transition to life away from sport—to not have a team to come to every single day. In my opinion, it is even harder to see that team every day in person, but not be on the team anymore.

I had a lot of proud moments just being on the sidelines and watching my sisters grow and dominate on the basketball floor. There were times they completely surprised me and times they humbled me. I will never forget an article written about Sierra Michaelis, my fellow small-town 1A teammate, and part of the article reads:

"Despite facing a lower tier of competition in high school, Michaelis never felt like she had to prove that she belonged in Division I. "Morgan Eye pretty much did that for me," said Michaelis, who was ready to commit to Nebraska before the Tigers—her dream school—swooped in during the eleventh hour." I'm just following in her footsteps."

Talk about a proud moment. Sierra Michaelis had a heck of a career at Mizzou and I am proud to say that I got to play with her for two years and watch from the sidelines for her last two years.

*** *** ***

**I graduated from the** University of Missouri with my Master's Degree in May 2017. The basketball season had ended and now life was really about to get real. Just when I thought I was getting a hold on my feelings and struggles of adjustment from not playing anymore, now it was time to think about what I was going to be doing next. Even more scary was WHERE I was going to be next.

I had many days where I just cried because I had no clue what I was going to do. Coach P always assured me that things were going to work out. It was just hard to feel like I was sitting around waiting for something to happen when I should be making something happen. When I really stopped to reflect about what I wanted to do, I knew I wanted to impact lives. I felt like I had acquired a lot of knowledge and wisdom through my experiences and basketball would be the perfect platform to share. That was when I knew I wanted to give coaching a shot.

As jobs opened up, Coach P helped me get into contact with who I needed to. She made many phone calls on my behalf and I knew that her word was well-respected in the basketball community. I knew I had a good person in my corner as I was trying to find my first coaching position. One opportunity came up and just when I let myself really start to picture myself there and get somewhat excited, it didn't pan out. It was a scary time not knowing where I was going to be working — or even if I was going to be working. Again, I had Coach P in my corner, because she paid me to stay as a G.A. for part of the summer session and help out with her camps. She was a life saver because it really helped with having to pay rent and such.

On the days when I felt the lowest, like there was no shot of me getting a job, I just prayed for God to help me trust in his plan. I would say to him with tears streaming down my face, "God, I know you have something planned for me. It is just really hard for me to see it right now."

That is the thing about faith, and my life story. I can't always see what is ahead of me, but I have to trust in God's plan. Just like with my basketball career, God's vision for my career was way better than anything I could have dreamed up on my own.

It was now time for me to trust that God would do the same for me with my job career.

# 34

Chapter

**O**pportunity **came up on** my Twitter feed one fine day. I set notifications on certain Twitter accounts to notify me when that particular account tweeted, and specifically this account that posted women's basketball coaching positions. I saw the words "Southeast Missouri State (SEMO) third assistant position" on the tweet. I immediately thought, "Hey, that's where Shep goes." My former teammate, Carrie Shephard, transferred after her sophomore season to SEMO. I played with Shep for one season and was a G.A. for the other season. I also thought how I would still be in Missouri and not too terribly far from home.

From there, Coach P worked her magic. She made some calls, put my name out there, and put in a good word for me. Rekha Patterson was the head coach at SEMO and was heading into her third year at the time. She was looking to fill the third assistant coach position and it seemed like it could be a good starting job for me. Throughout the process, Coach Patterson wanted to really get to know me, because she wanted to be sure she had the right fit for that position. We had multiple conversations on the phone. We talked basketball, but we also talked a lot about other things just to get to know one another. I enjoyed all of our conversations and always felt that they went really well. Coach Patterson let me know during one of our conversations that she would like for me to come down to Cape Girardeau, Missouri for an in-person interview. I was all for that, of course. She informed me that I was one of two candidates for the job.

I felt very confident, based solely on the multiple conversations we had over the phone.

I made the little three-hour drive to Cape Girardeau the night before my interview. I stayed at the Pear Tree Inn right off of the main highway, and I was so stoked because they provided complimentary popcorn and drinks in their hotel. I was so stoked about the popcorn — I get my love for popcorn from my mom — that I remember even Snapchatting Mike and my mom the popcorn I took to my room. I felt ready for my interview. I laid out my clothes and ironed them. I had bought a red shirt for my interview to wear with black pants and a black jacket, since I figured I couldn't go wrong with wearing SEMO colors. I had some downtime that evening, so I went ahead and made a SEMO women's basketball graphic to showcase what I could do. Coach Patterson had asked me to bring some of my Photoshop recruiting materials, so I had a portfolio of Mizzou stuff but wanted to add a personal touch.

For breakfast, I met Director of Basketball Operations Brooke Hengst, graduate-assistant Aisha Foy, and assistant coach Chante' Crutchfield. We made causal conversations over our meal, mostly talking about where everyone went to school and basic background information. The conversation shifted to the NBA Finals and what we expected would unfold in the upcoming games. They all seemed very nice and the conversation flowed easily.

After breakfast, I met with a lot of university administrators, Senior Women's Administrator Cindy Gannon, Dana Seabough with Admissions, and our Sports Information Director, Sean Livingston. They were all such great people and made me feel right at home. Then I met Coach Patterson, and she took me on the rest of the tour of the city of Cape Girardeau, which was similar to Columbia for me because it had a small-town feel but it was big enough that it had stuff to do. I was smitten about the downtown area. I just thought it was so cute and I loved the historic feel of it. The Missouri Wall of Fame along the Mississippi river was probably my favorite spot, along with going out to look at the river.

While at the basketball offices, one of the SEMO players stopped by. School was getting ready to start in a few days, so players were starting to get back into town. The player who made an appearance was none other than Carrie Shephard. I wish I had a video camera to capture her face when she saw me. It honestly was really awkward. I don't think she expected to see me, because I decided not to even tell her I was interviewing for the job even though I had just seen her the weekend prior at one of our teammates' wedding. She acted very quiet, which is very odd for Carrie. She did happen to make out the words to Coach Patterson, "Why y'all dressed up." Coach Patterson explained I was on an interview and I think then it made more sense to Carrie. It was a weird idea to think I could be coaching one of my former teammates, but it was an idea I very much welcomed.

After lunch, we finished the day with me showing my portfolio of graphics. They were all very impressed with my work, which made me feel really good about myself. I had come a long way from my first year of trying to do anything in Photoshop. After my short presentation, I had my one-on-one meeting with Coach Patterson. We sat in her office and she took me through her binder that she gives to the coaches. It outlines the program's values, mission, rules, guidelines, and more. I could tell by the way she spoke that she was someone who was passionate about what she does, has a vision for what she wants to get done, and has a relentless work ethic to get where she wants to be. Then she grilled me with a few different scenarios and asked how I would respond to those situations. I felt I answered them well and honestly. We wrapped up our talk and then I was headed out the door.

Overall, I thought the visit went really well and the people I met were real and genuine. For me, it wasn't about just getting a job but finding something that felt right for me. Just like Coach Patterson was looking for someone to be the "right fit," I knew I was doing the same thing. Coach Patterson was not at all worried about my lack of experience in coaching. She felt those types of things were all things I could learn, but it was more important for me to fit the program.

Before I drove home, I was able to respond to the good luck texts I received from some of my Mizzou family. I appreciated them thinking about me on my big day with my first job interview. I hadn't heard from Coach P though, which I thought was odd.

I then shot Carrie a text and asked her if I caught her off guard a little. She responded with the sweetest text ever, saying how she was so excited and really hoped that I got the job. She felt that I could really help them. I felt relieved reading her text because when I was there and she saw me, her reaction let off something different. She was texting me the very next day to find out if I got the job, but I only responded with the emoji with a zipper over its mouth.

Then I called Mike, Mom (who informs Dad) and my sister and gave everyone the play-by-play. I told them I felt very confident about how the day went and debated if I were to get offered the job that I may accept it on the spot because I didn't feel there was anything else for me to think about it. The job was my only opportunity at the time, it was a job in Missouri, it was a Division I coaching position, and I really enjoyed the people and my time during my visit. Coach Patterson said she would get back with me the next day.

I arrived back to Columbia around 6 o'clock. I went straight to the arena and sent thank you emails to everyone who I had met that day during my visit. Then I put on my workout clothes and got a good run in. Luckily, I had the weight room to myself and was able to hop on the treadmill and watch some basketball while I worked out. My phone buzzed as I was running and I looked down to see I had a message from Coach Putnam. I read the message and it said, "Not sure if anyone told you, but Robin's dad passed away." I remember hopping off the treadmill and just letting out a "no" and shaking my head. There had been a tragic accident. No one had said anything to me because I was on my interview and they didn't want me to be distracted. My first feeling was heartbreak for Coach P and her family. I couldn't begin to imagine what they all were going through. Then I felt like a selfish human being for even wondering "why hasn't Coach P texted me when she knew I had an interview?" Her world had just been shaken and I selfishly wanted to know why she wasn't thinking of me. Of course, there was no way for me to have known what was going on when I was miles away, but I still felt horrible. I immediately texted Coach P and her husband and sent my condolences and told them to let me know if there was anything I could do. I was simply in disbelief.

I went home after my workout and Skyped with Mike. We recapped our days. We talked about how my interview went and then, all of a sudden, my phone was ringing. It was Coach Patterson. I took the call and after talking about the how the interview went, Coach Patterson offered me the job. Knowing I had already talked to Mom, my sister, and Mike, I accepted the job right on the spot. I told Coach Patterson I would love to accept the position. I felt that everything was real and genuine on my visit and could really see myself there. I told her I didn't feel I needed any more time to think about it. Just like that, I had my very first job and coaching opportunity.

I called my parents right after and told them I accepted the job. I texted my sister and let them know I would be a Redhawk. I skyped Mike right back, gave a little smile, and said, "I took the job." Mike let out a big, "Yes! Let's goooo!" He was very excited for me and it felt good that he supported me. I was feeling good and then, all of a sudden, I had a wave of emotion sweep over me and I had to cover my laptop camera because I didn't want Mike to see me crying. (I am an ugly crier.)

The reality was hitting me hard in that moment that I was leaving Mizzou, a place I called home for six years. It was hard to believe it had been that long and I was saying goodbye. I laid in bed that night and reality just kept setting in—I couldn't believe I was going to be moving and starting a real job. I would be further from my hometown than I had ever been, nearly six hours.

I got up early the next day to go to the team individuals at Mizzou. I wanted to soak up all the knowledge I could before leaving. Everyone was asking me how the interview went and I told them I took it. I got a lot of hugs and congrats, but nothing really felt that great because we all knew the tragedy that had just happened with Coach P's father the night before. To no one's surprise, Coach Pingeton still came to workouts that morning. She came up to me and gave me a hug, and I wanted to hold on a little longer and tell her how sorry I was. Before I even got the chance, she asked me how the job interview went. I told her I accepted it. She was happy for me. I don't think I have ever met a stronger, more selfless person than Coach P.

Weeks passed, and my time at Mizzou dwindled. On my last day, Coach P and I spent a little time together before I made my official move to Cape Girardeau. We decided to go for a stroll. Our first stop was in Mizzou Arena on the main court. We made small-talk about my career and then Coach said, "Well, you have to make one more shot." I went to the right wing behind the 3-point line, I lined up to my target, and shot ... just short. I tried once more. Short again. Okay, so here's the thing, I had flip flops, on so I kicked those off and I needed to compensate for not having a basketball shoe on. There was no way I was going to miss a third. I picked up my target one more time, and swished it. I put my flip flops back on and gave Coach P a high-five. We continued our walk outside on the trail just behind Mizzou Arena. We talked about a little bit of everything. It was fun to get some one-on-one time with Coach. I have always enjoyed our talks, and this time I wasn't sweating bullets like I would have been as a player. There was no denying I would miss Coach P a great deal. She was a big reason why I decided to try coaching. She had such a great impact on my life that I knew I wanted to help others in the same way.

As we made it back to the arena, I gave my last hugs to everyone and turned in my keys. Those keys had gotten me into the gym many times to get in extra shots, to come to an early conditioning workout, to lift weights, to get food from the locker room or to take a nap. It was weird how much lighter my key chain was now. Before I walked to the elevator, I handed Coach P a letter I had written the night before. I knew there was more I wanted to say to her than what would be said during our walk. I left the letter with her and walked to the elevator.

> *Coach P,*
> *You walked into the gym on Tuesday the 13th, not even a full day after finding out the news about your father and you asked with a smile how my interview went. I wanted to hold on to your hug just a little*

273

*bit longer and tell you how sorry I was for your loss. Instead, you asked me multiple questions about the visit and I was just fighting back tears. I know I never said it to your face but only through text how sorry I am about your dad. He really was a special guy and I will miss seeing him.*

*I could make the assumption that maybe you asked about my interview to take your mind off of things but I know that it's because you just truly care about others. You always put others before yourself. I know you never like people to ask "how you're doing" because when faced with adversity you only know to*

Getting hired as an assistant coach at Southeast Missouri was a perfect first job for me. I loved our staff and Cape Girardeau, because it reminded me a lot of Columbia.

*roll up your sleeves and go back to work — just like your dad taught you. I hope one day to only be a quarter of the coach, wife, mother, and mentor you are. You are truly amazing and the cool part is, you don't even realize it.*

*There is no depth, detail, or length of letter that could possibly thank you for what you have done for me in my life. From giving me a chance to live out my dream of division I basketball, to continuing to be around the program as a G.A., and then helping me find a job. I am so blessed to have met you and to have you in my life. I don't know what it is about you but you have always had the power to make my day whether it was a short conversation in the halls or a wink when you passed by. I respect, care, and love you probably more than you will ever know. I am forever grateful for EVERYTHING that you have done for me in my life. Thank you for pushing me to be the best that I could be. Thank you for believing in me. I love you Coach P.*

*Mo*

# 35

Chapter

**As it was time for me** to move on to the next chapter of my life, another big event was about to take place. Mike and I had been dating for nearly two years and had been through a lot together. I had told Mike before that he was truly my saving grace when I felt completely alone that first year as a G.A. He was in a similar boat as his friends were graduating and moving to other cities. We truly built our relationship on friendship. Because of that, I have to share just a few of my more notable stories of our relationship that make me laugh.

Before Mike and I officially started dating, we hung out a lot just as friends. One of the first instances when I knew Mike was going to be a keeper was the night he showed up in a surprising manner at my apartment door. We had spent an evening with friends in a casual setting at a bar. We just had some drinks and watched some sports. Mike and I got to talking about the evening and what we like to do. Mike didn't really care for that particular setting and felt like sometimes he just wanted to hang out with some of his buddies. I totally understood, but I started to feel a sense of worry because a bunch of things that he described as not really being "his thing" I thought those were "my things."

I got a little nervous about what our future would look like if we don't enjoy doing some of the same things. I like having a casual beer and relaxing with friends talking about nothing. I was probably fretting about nothing but Mike wanted to make sure my mind was put at ease. The next evening, I left work and at my apartment I heard an unexpected knock. I opened the door to Mike standing in the doorway blaring Eric Church's song "Drink in My Hand" and chugging a Bud Light bottle. I just smiled and shook my head. This guy hates beer and here he is trying to make me feel better. I can't remember exactly what he said, but it was along the lines of doing anything to make me happy. I know, he is sweeter than I deserve. I was still in such disbelief. I think the only words I made out was, "You don't have to finish that," and reached out to grab the beer — and yes, I finished it.

\*\*\*   \*\*\*   \*\*\*

**M**y sister and her husband do a dance known as the "Pretzel" and I have always thought it was a really cool dance. I told Mike I wanted to learn it, and so we got on YouTube and learned the dance. It took countless times practicing in my small apartment living room and a couple of test runs at the downtown bar Nash Vegas to finally master it, but we did it.

We whip out the dance any time we feel the beat. One of my most favorite times was in downtown Columbia in the middle of a street in the middle of the night. We could hear the music, so we went with it. We still get rusty now and then, but muscle memory soon takes over and we are back to moving swiftly.

\*\*\*   \*\*\*   \*\*\*

**B**eing in an interracial relationship, I have a lot of fun coming up with ideas when it is time to dress up for an event. For our first Halloween together, Taylor Swift and Kanye West got costumed up for the evening and hit the town in Columbia.

My personal favorite was a Pub Crawl Golf tour

we went to in which "golf attire" was encouraged. Golf attire? Okay, I got you. I managed to borrow a Pittsburgh Penguins hockey jersey and Mike found a yellow pull-over and golf hat at our local Goodwill and we went as Happy Gilmore and Chubbs. I won't forget the looks we got walking downtown Columbia and seeing people crack a smile when it occurred to them who we were dressed like.  I will accept any and all ideas for future outfits. Thank you.

*** *** ***

Mike has called me an onion before, meaning you just have to keep pulling back my layers. I think I put up more walls than I am willing to admit at times. However, I was finally ready to bring down the biggest wall and say the words "I love you" to Mike. He had said he loved me maybe three other times and I just wasn't ready to do it then. Months later, I was ready. I knew I wanted it to be meaningful. Ideally, I thought I would do it in Mizzou Arena. It seemed like the perfect spot because we met at Mizzou, he was a scout guy and I played, and Mizzou really brought us together. Unfortunately, it was gradu-ation weekend when I wanted to do it. Commencement ceremonies were taking place in the main arena, and even the practice gym was crowded.

Mike was headed home with me for the big Memo-rial Day weekend celebrations, so I thought of a different plan. I would tell Mike I love him on the St. Mary's out-door court in Montrose—the same court I grew up on just across the street from Grandma's house.

It was mid-afternoon on a Saturday and we were hanging out with friends near St. Mary's. We saw some of my cousins shooting hoops, so we went and joined in for a little while. After a while, my cousins went across the street to my Grandma's and so Mike and I were left alone for a short period of time on the court.

My moment had come. I got Mike's attention and told him I had something I wanted to tell him. I told him how I had this master plan, but it didn't work. I told him how this court meant so much to me and was such a big part of me developing into who I am and bringing me to where I am today. It was special to share it with him — I wouldn't just bring anyone to my hometown. I explained to Mike how I had this elaborate plan to say the words "I love you." I told him that "I wanted to tell you some-where special that I love you. So what I am saying is, I love you." It was probably even more awkward than I recall, but the message ultimately got across.

*** *** ***

As with any relationship that takes a turn toward the "serious" path, sex is a topic that is obviously going to come up. As my relationship with Mike got more serious, I got more nervous about talking about sex. I guess I need to back up for this to make sense...

I have gone back and forth a lot about sharing this particular part of my story. It is a part of my life that is very private, but when I think about it, I want this book to be real and hide nothing. I asked a few of my friends about sharing and they also thought it important — and possibly even valuable — for young kids to hear.

So here I am in my most vulnerable state.

I am 26 years old — and I am a virgin.

I only share this part of my life because I think a lot of kids get the wrong impression of what they feel like they HAVE to do in high school or what the college scene looks like.

I am here to tell you your experiences are what you

make them. I had a serious boyfriend in high school and I asked my sister about helping me get on birth control because I knew I had to be on that or I would be constantly paranoid about getting pregnant and then not being able to play basketball. That is something that has always been in my mind—a young couple can get pregnant, but realistically a guy can hide that he is going to be a teen father, but for a woman it is one thing for everyone to see. Luckily, I had a very good and wise older sister who told me, "Morgan, you are too young." So I reluctantly waited until I was old enough to get birth control on my own. I finally reached the age of 18 but fell "out of love" with my boyfriend at the time. He was a great guy and we will always share the memories of a lot of firsts together. But I think we both knew deep down that we both needed to move on. He was leaving for college and I still had a year of high school left.

I didn't date at all my entire senior year of high school. I "talked" to a couple guys here and there, whatever that means in high school. I never went on any dates, but rather I just focused on school and basketball. I enjoyed the freedom of getting to do what I wanted. To some that may sound selfish, but when you are in high school, it is a time to enjoy being independent and enjoy being with friends. You have the rest of your life ahead of you to devote all of your time and energy to your spouse and kids. Personally, I never wanted to be in a relationship that meant you sacrificed an opportunity to be with friends because you felt you HAD to spend every last waking hour together with your boyfriend. Luckily when I dated in high school, my boyfriend and I shared the same group of friends, so it was always a win-win. I think the key is balance. I am not saying kids shouldn't date, because dating can be a very fun, nerve-wracking, and exciting time. I still remember getting butterflies in the early times of dating every time I held my boyfriend's hand. So again, it's all about balance, which I know especially as a teenager can be a hard concept to fully grasp.

I guess my words of wisdom for high schoolers is to never feel pressured into doing something you are not ready for. We see all the time in movies and television how sex is glamorized and people brag about how young they were when they first "did it." Because of that stigma, I believe people feel ashamed to be a virgin because it goes against what appears to be the norm. There are a variety of reasons why young kids have sex these days, and I believe one of them to be that they feel that they have to do it because everyone else is doing it. Well, I am sharing my story because I am not everyone.

Most, if not all, of my hometown friends knew about my virginity and I think they all respected me for it. But then it was time to head off to college and having people learn of my virginity really frightened me — especially people who I did not know well. Early on in college, my new friends were my teammates. We spent tons of time together, both at the arena and at the upperclassmen's apartments. I had only known my teammates for probably a few days and I could feel myself get hot and clammy any time the topic of sex came up because I just knew I would get asked questions and I didn't want to answer them.

The night came when my fellow freshmen and I went over to some of our teammates' apartment. The night was laid back, and we were just getting to know one another. Then I got asked point blank, "Mo, are you a virgin?" I know my body immediately got hot, but I was not about to lie — there was no reason to. I just replied, "Yeah, I am." Their reactions were not at all what I think I had built up in my head. I imagined bug-eyed, jaw-dropping reactions, but instead it was opposite. I think I feared getting made fun of or them giving me a hard time. Instead, they were like, "You definitely need to wait for someone you love." I completely felt the same way and was actually very relieved to not feel like I had to be awkward any time the topic of sex came up.

Sure, as time went on there would be little jokes here and there made about my virginity, but it has all been in good fun and has not bothered me at all. The older I get, the more mature I get and know how much I respect myself and my body and feel my decision to wait is the right thing. I was never about to have sex just to say I did it. Having sex is something sacred and I know I want to be in love. I am Catholic and so our beliefs as a community are that you are to wait until marriage to have sex. I am not perfect. I think I would be lying if I said the reason I have waited to have sex is solely because of the Commandment. It is part of the reason, but again, I can't say I am perfect. At the end of the day I know I want to be in love. I know that I have to be ready, he has to be ready, and the relationship has to be ready.

When I prayed to God about finding a great guy, I asked for tons of great qualities and one of those was that the man he sends me respects me and loves the fact that I respect myself.

God answered my prayers and sent me the perfect man. Mike Scott has been all that I could have prayed for and even more.

*** *** ***

**S**o now that I have shared a little bit of my relationship with Mike and my history with dating, I now want to share one of the biggest days of our lives together.

On August 5, 2017 Michael August Scott Jr. asked me to spend the rest of my life with him. I, of course, said yes.

I won't share all the details of the day because most of the day we spent fighting. It's actually kind of funny because you picture a day like that being so picture perfect, but it was far from it. That is life and that is relationships and that is what makes it feel so real. But let me indulge you all in the actual "fantasy" part because hey, it's my story and I can exclude any inconsequential details I want.

Mike and I had driven up to Kansas City for the weekend. All I wanted to do for my birthday was go see my Kansas City Royals for the first time that season. We ended up at my cousin Kendall's new apartment — just in time for Mike to help move some furniture up a flight of stairs. After Kendall was settled into her apartment, Mike asked if I wanted to open my birthday present. I had completely forgotten about it, but wanted my gift, so we ran down to the car to get it. I sat down on the couch with the shoebox-sized gift on my lap. My friend Eric got up

Mike got creative when it finally came time to ask me to marry him, using a new pair of shoes to tie the engagement to my Cinderella story.

from the couch to stand over to my right and Kendall was standing in the middle of the living room on her phone. Mike stood there to my left, watching me as I began tearing the paper. The torn paper revealed a Kobe Bryant shoe box. I flipped the lid open to find my very first pair of Kobes!

This is a huge deal because I have zero shoe game! Everyone probably wants to know the year, the type etc. but guess what, I can't even tell you that! I will tell you they were beautifully white and I liked them a lot. I began picking the brown paper out of the shoes so that I could put them on. Then I came across a little brown bag, which I thought was a try-on disposable sock, and I said, "Oh," and then tossed the bag to Mike, who happened to be on one knee right in front of me.

I quickly realized what was going on. Mike had prepared a sweet little speech that related back to my dream of playing Division I basketball and living out my Cinderella story. He remembered me telling the story in my senior banquet speech how, "I ain't gonna be no Cinderella," turned into me living my fairytale. Down on his knee as he took the ring out of the brown felt bag, he said, "I know you aren't Cinderella or anything, but if the shoe fits, would you marry me?" I sat there in awe, pointed toward my right and said, "Is that why Eric's been recording this whole time?" I thought it was super weird how he got up as soon as I sat down to open my present. Then I made out the word "Yes!"

It's funny how patience has been a theme in my life. I had to be patient for my opportunity to get a Division I scholarship offer. I had to be patient in my development as a basketball player. I had to be patient in my personal life in waiting for the right man.

Patience is hard. But patience is worth it!

*** *** ***

As cliché as it is, when I tell my life story I cannot help but encourage everyone to DREAM BIG! When I was maybe a freshman in high school, we were all standing in the lunch line that curled out the doors and into the hallways. Conversations about basketball were circling as we inched closer to the doors to enter the tiny lunch room. I made the comment about wanting to play college basketball when I graduated from high school. One of my friends made a face with an eye roll as to say, "There is no way you are good enough to play in college." Judging by the reaction, I quickly followed my words with, "Um, like a small school somewhere." The friend's reaction changed to a more understanding one because I guess this time my words made a little more sense.

How much sweeter it would have been if I had stuck my shoulders back and just said, "WATCH ME!" Instead, I belittled my own dream because I was afraid of what someone else thought about me.

Your dreams are your dreams. I also think with having a dream you have to also be realistic about what gifts God gave you. If I were to say it is my dream to be the next big singer, I would not mind if you laughed in my face because I was not blessed with great singing ability. What I was blessed with, was an ability to play basketball, an incredible work ethic, desire to be better, and a lot more, which allowed me to live out my dream.

So, when thinking about what your dreams truly are, I believe you have to think about what God is calling you to do. I know my story is not completely written, but God did help me live out one of my childhood dreams of playing Division I basketball and doing it at my home-state school Mizzou.

*** *** ***

**N**o matter how hard you think you worked in high school, it is nothing compared to what you are going to experience at the college level. To be a high-level athlete, you truly have to feed your body the right stuff. You have to feed yourself good stuff physically, mentally, spiritually, and emotionally — it is all encompassing.

In college, you may have an early morning workout, go to class, then come back for a shooting session, grab lunch, go to class, come back for workouts, grab food, meet with tutors, study – and then do it all again the next day. The crazy thing though, your body CAN do it. I loved this saying that I heard, "Sometimes we have to TALK to ourselves, instead of LISTENING to ourselves." The translation of that can be related to those times when your body starts to feel fatigued and mentally you just want to check out and be done because you are a little uncomfortable. It is in those moments when you have to stop listening to those thoughts and start speaking the right thoughts in your head.

*** *** ***

**I** will be the first to admit that I like to enjoy a beer, a glass of wine, a cocktail or whatever every once in a while. Where I am in the stage in my life now, it is perfectly fine for me to enjoy those things. However, I have learned that it is not the best thing in the world, like I used to think as a younger adult. I used to think how cool it will be to be old enough to buy beer and to buy drinks at a bar.

I actually got really lucky in high school. Following the night of our basketball Homecoming game, the same night I was crowned Homecoming Queen my junior year, I joined my friends at a party. We had planned it for weeks. We were going to have an after-party, and there would be drinking. We had it all planned in a safe way so no one would be drinking and driving.

I arrived after the dance concluded. I had about a beer and a half and in walks two Missouri State Patrol officers. I remember the two officers with their broad-brimmed hats walk in and tell us to turn off the music. I think everyone was in shock because no one moved to turn off the music. The officer told us once again, but this time with more authority, to turn off the music. I was just trying to wrap my mind around the reality that this was actually happening. All I could think about was "What does this mean for basketball season?" We were not letting anyone drive, we thought we were being responsible. Responsible or not, it was not in accordance with the law. Luckily, most of us got off scot-free. For others, it meant being restricted from playing a number of basketball games.

Both the boys and girls basketball teams had to run 1,000 lines for the party. If you were at the party, you ran 1,000 lines. If you weren't, you still ran 500. I learned quickly that drinking was not the most important thing in the world to me. I wanted to play ball, plain and simple. I didn't drink at all my senior year in high school because I knew what the consequences could hold. It only takes ONE time, and ONE mistake to really mess things up. That evening was a blessing to me for sure. And guess what, my senior year was still a blast! My friends and I found plenty of ways to still have fun and make memories without drinking.

As I went off to college, I definitely enjoyed the social party scene. I worked hard and played hard, so to speak. I don't think there is necessarily anything wrong with that, as long as you are smart and safe. If you party, make sure you have a way home. If you party, make sure you are with people you know and trust. As much as I did enjoy to let loose on the weekends, I never did so once the basketball season started. In fact, I never went out on a weeknight to party until the last game of my career was played. While drinking in the offseason didn't do my body good, I knew I especially didn't want to hinder my performance during the regular season. I knew I wanted to perform at my absolute best, and choosing to drink and party during season would have seemed selfish to me.

Like a lot of things in life, it comes down to balance.

*** *** ***

**I** **quickly learned in college** that I had to think about my teammates, my coaches, and my family before making decisions. Anything that I did was a direct reflection of the university I played for, our women's basketball program, and my family. I always wanted to do my very best for those people in my life. When you play or work for something that is bigger than yourself, you will be able to accomplish way more than you ever thought possible. Be "others" focused. There were times I wanted to make selfish decisions, but I had to think about how that would affect others around me. There were also times when I focused on others that it pushed me past walls of exhaustion. When I focused on playing for someone else and being the best teammate I could be, I was able to play even harder. I was not playing to glorify my name. I was playing to help others.

I was first introduced to the idea of playing for an audience of One (playing for God) when I attended Fellowship of Christian Athletes meetings. I'm sure everyone has their own interpretation of what that means to them. For me, it means doing my absolute best with the gifts God gave me and giving Him the praise and not wanting it for my own human satisfaction. It means never fearing failure. I can go out and trust that if I do my best, all will work itself out.

My advice: don't do things for your own selfish satisfaction. Be a servant to others, be others focused. *"For what profit is it to a man if he gains the whole world, and loses his soul?" — Matthew 16:26*

*** *** ***

**I**t's funny how many kids go off to college and do laundry for the first time in their lives. I was one of them. It's one of those small things that we may easily take for granted until it's our turn to be responsible, because my mom did my laundry every time before I went to college.

But when it was time to go home for break or a quick weekend, I definitely brought home my dirty laundry. I don't think Mom even minded one bit because I was back home. I would take my clean and perfectly folded laundry back to college and just smell it — maybe I wasn't doing my laundry right because it never smelled that good!

Over the course of my college years, I can't tell you how many times my friends and I said the phrase, "Well that's how my Mom/Dad does it." This covered a variety of things, from cooking, to grilling, doing dishes, washing clothes, hanging things on the wall, yard work, car mechanics, and so much more. Any question my friends or I couldn't figure out, it was a quick call to Mom or Dad to see how to do it.

To kids heading off to college, just listen to yourself when you are making one of your favorite family dishes and a friend asks about one of your techniques or what you put in it. When you are fixing something around the house and your friend asks how you knew how to do it, you may be very surprised how often you say, "Well, that's how my Mom/Dad does it." To Mom and Dad: See, I listen.

*** *** ***

**I**'ll **never forget after** a few years at Mizzou and having broken a few records, I was chatting with a hometown friend, Corey Brownsberger, via Facebook Messenger. It was mostly small talk and just catching up. Before we closed the conversation, Corey said, "Morgan, you are still you." I remember thinking, "Of course, I am still me. I will never forget where I grew up and where I come from."

I am not sure if others thought I would get a big head or become "too good" to come back home because of some of the success that I experienced at Mizzou. Even at the ages of 18 and 20, I think I was raised to have a level head and to be humble. Did it feel good to have my name in the newspaper and talked about? Absolutely. It did not, however, change who I was as a person.

I know I am where I am today because of where I came from, where I was raised, and how I was raised. Montrose couldn't keep me from coming back home. I always had a countdown to the next time I got to cruise down the main street in Montrose and just be home. When people ask me how things are back home, my typical response is, "Not much has changed … but that is exactly how I like it."

Home is always something that I can count on.

*** *** ***

**I was blessed with** some really amazing teammates throughout my entire career. The best friend I made during my college experience was Bree Fowler. I mentioned early on in this book that I could literally write a complete other book just about this girl because she is that amazing. Bree is an amazing listener, and I learned that early on in our friendship. I would tell her stories about my family and weeks later when I am telling another story about them, she would rattle off their names as if she was related to them, too.

Bree was that teammate that every girl could confide in. Bree knew everything about everyone and it was not because she was a gossip or that she sought out information. It was simply because everyone really trusted Bree and she was such a great listener. I remember a time after one of our games, Bree and I sat in our car parked in the loading dock. I had been struggling for a couple of games and practices in a row and I finally just let it all out. I was bawling. I was so frustrated with how I had been playing and she knew it was eating at me so she just listened. Coach P always explained it to us girls like this, "It's like vomiting. It makes you feel better, but doesn't do much for the other person." Bree let me vomit on her that night and many other times as well. She is a very selfless person and I am blessed to call her a best friend. We laughed a lot together and cried a lot together.

Bree and I came to Mizzou as freshman and we left as seniors. We shared many firsts and many lasts. We were probably what you would consider an unlikely friendship had we not been brought together by the beautiful game of basketball. I was from a small town, she was from Kansas City, I love country music, she loves hip-hop, I am white, she is black. Her mom said we were, "Salt & Pepper." We have been rolling with that ever since. Bree Fowler is my rock, and I am hers. I would do anything for her. I always look forward to seeing her and reminiscing about our days at Mizzou. Now, we sit back and look at the Mizzou women's basketball program and proudly say we played a big part in laying the foundation.

*** *** ***

As much as I thought Coach P was crazy when she sat me down on her couch in her office my senior year of high school and told me that my teammates would become my best friends, she was actually right. I always thought, I have best friends already and they are my childhood friends and cousins who I've known all of my life. There was no way she was trying to tell me that I could possibly form that same bond over just a few years. She was right, though. My teammates became my sisters.

A memory that I will forever cherish was the summer going into my junior season when our team decided we wanted to do a camping trip and decided Montrose would be the best place to do it. I don't think the girls knew what to expect coming to my small town, but I was

We had so much fun as a team heading back to my hometown for a fun little camping weekend.

so happy to have them experience it all. I remember my
Mom being excited but also nervous just making sure
we had enough food, and food everyone liked, and that
everyone just felt welcomed. As the date approached for
my team and I to head home, my mom told me, "Tell the
girls we can't promise they will have a good time, but I
promise they will be fed." I think my Mom went over-
board with the snacks but hey, girls gotta eat.

The trip was just a one-night adventure. We got to
Montrose in the afternoon and I showed the girls around
my house. Then we quickly jumped in our vehicles to
head to my sister's house just about twenty-five minutes
away in Lowry City. There we would all pile in pick-up
trucks with our swim-floaties, and then head to the "pit."
I put quotations around "pit" because I came to find that
no one knew what I was talking about when I would
explain how my hometown friends and I go swimming at
the pits.

Basically, the "pit" is a small body of water. I always
explain it as bigger than a pond, but smaller than a lake.
It's called a pit because it is an old strip-mining pit that
workers used to dig for coal. The particular pit I was
taking our team to is the best one I have ever been to. My
brother-in-law had been going there since he was a kid. It
has the clearest water, beautiful cliffs and trees, and even
a picnic table area.

I made sure to warn the girls that the fish do start to
bite when it gets closer to sunset. Maddie Stock found
that out first-hand. She was sitting in a donut inflatable
and mid-conversation let out a big howl and thrust her
hips forward to get her butt out of the water. Once the fish
start biting means it's time to call it a day.

The evening consisted of a bonfire and some amazing home-cooked food. We enjoyed getting to hang out
with one another and just be outdoors. I will say that the

"camping" part was glamorized with the use of some campers. Some of the girls even ended up inside the house asleep on the couch. It was still a very fun evening and my sister woke up the team with some of her amazing homemade cinnamon rolls from Grandma Jackie's recipe.

I don't think I could ever express to my teammates how much it meant to me that they wanted to come to my hometown. But not only did they want to come just that once, but we made the trip once again my senior year. This time we made team T-shirts that read "Time for a 'PIT' stop." And this go-around I made sure to show the team all of the "hot spots" in town. I showed them my high-school, my Grandma Jackie's house, our church, our Catholic grade school that basically my entire family attended, Short Street (the best restaurant in town), and we stopped to pose for pictures with locals who were out mowing their lawn.

We again went to the pit for some good afternoon swimming. It was just as fun as I had remembered it the first time. After finishing swimming, we headed back to my house for dinner. We decided it was smarter to just go back home instead of trying to "camp" again. There was plenty of space at my house and that way everyone could shower if they wanted to and just enjoy a nice evening.

I have always been proud of where I come from. It was quite the honor to get to share a piece of me that is so important and I got to share it with people I love. To my teammates, you are always welcome to visit Montrose any time! We would all love to have you. Whether you want to grab dinner at Short Street, swim in the pits, or hang out at my house, you will always be welcomed. And if you can't remember how to get to my house, just ask a stranger (probably a relative) walking down the street and they will point where you need to go.

*** *** ***

$M$y basketball career was definitely not what I thought it would be. Actually, my ENTIRE college experience was nothing that I ever thought it would be. I had thoughts of what it may be like and even had dreams of the success I could experience. However, God's plan for me was way better than anything I could ever dream up on my own.

Remember after the Cleveland Cavaliers won their first NBA title and LeBron James said, "I'm just this kid from Akron. I'm not even supposed to be here." Well, if I may, "I'm just this kid from Montrose. I'm not even supposed to be here." How did a girl from a town of just 384 people, graduate from her high school class of 12, become the best three-point shooter in the University of Missouri women's basketball history? I did things like break records at Mizzou with most career three-pointers made, most threes made in a season (also an SEC record), most three-pointers made in a game, led the NCAA in three-pointers made per game, named the Southeastern Conference co-sixth Woman of the Year, invited to the USA World University Games, and participated in the State Farm College Three-Point Competition. These were all things I certainly did not dream up when thinking of what my college experience might be like but God blessed me anyway.

All of that would not have even been close to possible if it had not been for the amazing people in my life. First, a huge thank you to my parents, my sister, and all my family and friends. Whether I broke a record at Mizzou or never saw a minute of playing time, I know their unconditional love would not waiver. My parents modeled firsthand what hard work looked like and always pushed me to do my best in whatever I pursued. My sister, my role model, was always there to pick me up when I am down and always there to keep my head on straight. My family and friends have always supported me and made the trip to Columbia many times to do so in person.

A thank you to all of my high school coaches over my career (basketball, softball, and cross country included). You all impacted my life more than you probably know. Please continue to positively impact the lives of students that come across your path. I know I am forever grateful for what you have done for me. It's amazing how things come full circle. I remember back to high school, and one time when I missed a shot, it rolled over to Coach Ireland. He threw it back to me and said, "You don't have to chase them if you make them." I laugh because that's something I say to my girls at Southeast Missouri today.

Uncle Kent, thank you for investing so much time into those young little girls who dreamed of winning a state championship. Thank you for your time, energy, and commitment to us. Thank you for the memorable limo drives, weekend tournaments, and McDonald's runs. I hope you realize that winning Montrose's first ever state championship or my dream of playing at Mizzou would not have been possible had you not INVESTED in me. Thank you, and I love you!

I would like to send a special thank you to Tom Brew of Hilltop30 Publishing Group who helped me write, edit, and bring this book to life. I would not have been able to do this without you. We made a great team! Thank you!

And lastly, thank you to Coach P and all of my coaches for taking a chance on a kid no one had heard of. Thank you for your investment in my life. Thank you for pushing me day in and day out to be my absolute best. You helped me become the best basketball player I could be and the best person I could be.

I am still learning and growing and because of you, I

am now helping other young ladies do the same as I step into the role of coaching. Thank you for being the best example of what a coach should be like. Every day in my new job, I take things that I learned from Coach P and her great staff at Mizzou.

Just recently, I had a senior player at SEMO who was struggling, and it took me straight back to how Coach P helped me get through my slump my senior year. I shared that story, and it helped. And then I shared how Coach P prayed for me, and Coach Patterson then asked me if I would pray with our player. Of course I said yes, and we gathered together and held hands as I prayed. I could feel the heat rushing through my body, that at that moment I was doing EXACTLY what I was put on this earth to do. I was praying, and I was helping, just like so many other coaches had done for me.

It was a miracle moment.

My life, amazingly, had come full circle.

# Epilogue — Dear Basketball

*Dear basketball,*

*I don't think I can begin to explain the amazing blessings that you have brought into my life. From a very young age, you came into my world and forever changed it. From a little tomboy to a grown woman, you have been there every step of the way.*

*You were a childhood friend. I played with you every day. You brought me and my friends closer together. We wanted so badly to compete and be the best because of you. You kept me working hard, you kept me disciplined, you kept me striving for more.*

*You brought the entire community of Montrose, Missouri together every basketball season to show support. Sometimes you broke our hearts, but we always and continue to come back for more. You let us feel the high of winning a championship and feel the pride in singing our school song, "Let us make her the best in the state alright!" You helped forever link my childhood friends and I together, and we always have basketball memories to share.*

*You paid for my college education. I have a Bachelor's degree from the University of Missouri in Business Marketing, and a Master's Degree in Educational Counseling, Schooling, and Psychology, with an Emphasis in Positive Coaching.*

*You helped me live out my dream of playing Division I basketball and do so for my home state at the University of Missouri. Because of you, I met so many diverse people. I got to play for the BEST coaches in the world. I got to meet and play with the BEST teammates anyone could ever ask for. I traveled to so many places because of you. I rode on private planes and jets like it was a normal routine and even sat in the cockpit as a co-pilot. I played in historic basketball venues all around the* nation. I played against future WNBA professional women's basketball players. I met future Hall of Fame coaches. I've seen a lot and I am not done yet.

I met my future husband because of you. Basketball, you continue to be the talking point between Mike and me. In fact, you are almost all we talk about. You are kind of like having a kid. On dinner dates, we have to remind ourselves, "Okay, no talking about basketball (the kids)." Thank you for bringing Mike into my world.

Basketball, you taught me a lot about going out and fighting for what I want. I remember Kara Lawson saying to the group of girls at the USA trials, "What I love about the game of basketball is that the game doesn't lie. You can always tell who put in the work." Thank you, basketball, for always being honest. For making me prove my hard work and skills. You never made it easy but you made it worth it.

I have a job because of you. I get to impact the lives of young ladies through teaching the game of basketball. Thank you for making me a student of the game and for graduating me to be a teacher.

Basketball, I could probably go on forever thanking you. The impact you have had on my life is immeasurable. Above all, thank you for the amazing people and relationships you have brought into my life. Without the relationships, none of this would be worth it. Thank you for allowing me to live out my Cinderella story. But with you, basketball, the clock never strikes 12 – the fairytale never ends. My book is not closed. I am now just on a new chapter.

I hope I held up my end of the bargain. I felt it was my responsibility to give you my all. Basketball, I hope I made you proud.

**With love,**
**Morgan "Mo" Eye #30**